Epworth Comme

General E
Ivor H. J

The Book of Exo

The Book of
EXODUS

Richard Coggins

EPWORTH PRESS

0 7162 0536 X

First published 2000
by Epworth Press
20 Ivatt Way
Peterborough, PE3 7PG

Typeset by Regent Typesetting, London
and printed in Great Britain by
Biddles Ltd, Guildford and King's Lynn

CONTENTS

GENERAL INTRODUCTION

The *Epworth Preacher's Commentaries* that Greville P. Lewis edited so successfully in the 1950s and 1960s having now served their turn, the Epworth Press has commissioned a team of distinguished academics who are also preachers and teachers to create a new series of commentaries that will serve readers into the twenty-first century. We have taken the opportunity offered by the publication in 1989 of the Revised English Bible to use this very readable and scholarly version as the basis of our commentaries, and we are grateful to the Oxford and Cambridge University Presses for the requisite licence and for granting our authors generous access. They will nevertheless be free to cite and discuss other translations wherever they think that these will illuminate the original text.

Just as the books that make up the Bible differ in their provenance and purpose, so our authors will necessarily differ in the structure and bearing of their commentaries. But they will all strive to get as close as possible to the intention of the original writers, expounding their texts in the light of the place, time, circumstances, and culture that gave them birth, and showing why each work was received by Jews and Christians into their respective Canons of Holy Scripture. They will seek to make full use of the dramatic advance in biblical scholarship world-wide but at the same time to explain technical terms in the language of the common reader, and to suggest ways in which Scripture can help towards the living of a Christian life today. They will endeavour to produce commentaries that can be used with confidence in ecumenical, multiracial, and multifaith situations, and not by scholars only but by preachers, teachers, students, church members, and anyone who wants to improve his or her understanding of the Bible.

PREFACE

There are numerous people whose help in writing this commentary
I should wish to acknowledge. First of all there were groups of
students at Kings College London; together we wrestled with the
Hebrew text of chapters 1–15. Then I should mention two very lively
seminars which I have been privileged to lead since my retirement:
one at Winchester, organized by Canon Keith Walker; the other at
Ludlow, for the Continuing Ministerial Education Programme of the
Anglican diocese of Hereford, organized by Will Pridie. A debt of
even longer standing is owed to Dr Cyril Rodd: many years ago he
earned my admiration and appreciation for his careful draft translation of Exodus for the 'Translators' Translation' sponsored by the
British and Foreign Bible Society, and more recently he approached
me to undertake this commentary for the Epworth Commentary
Series. To all these, together with Dr Ivor Jones and the Revd Gerald
Burt of the Epworth Press, I owe my thanks. They have all helped me
to organize my thoughts; the infelicities and errors that remain I claim
as my own.

Richard Coggins
Lymington
September 1999

ABBREVIATIONS

AV   Authorized Version

DOTT   *Documents from Old Testament Times*, edited by D.W.
            Thomas (Thomas Nelson 1958, and later reprints)

ET   English Translation

JSOT SS   Journal for the Study of the Old Testament: Supplement
            Series

LXX   The Septuagint Greek Translation of the Hebrew Bible

MT   Masoretic Text of the Hebrew Bible

NEB   New English Bible

NRSV   New Revised Standard Version

REB   Revised English Bible

RSV   Revised Standard Version

RV   Revised Version

INTRODUCTION

The Book of Exodus is a strange mixture. Its first half offers us an exciting story of the escape from Egypt of a group of slaves, under the human leadership of Moses but with God pictured as playing an active role. They reach a holy mountain, Sinai, and are given commandments to shape and guide their life. But at that point the story seems to lose momentum. Instead of making further progress on their journey to the land which has been promised to them as their goal, they become involved in the detailed preparation of religious impedimenta. This is described in what to many modern readers will seem intolerable detail, and the book ends with a religious task – the construction of the tabernacle – completed, but no further progress made on their journey.

How are we to read such a book? Very many different approaches have been proposed. For the early Christian community the story of the Exodus was seen as prefiguring the life, death and resurrection of Jesus. In the New Testament this is most specifically claimed at Luke 9. 31, though REB, like most modern translations, uses the word 'departure' rather than translate the Greek *exodon* literally. At about the same time as the New Testament was written the Jewish writer Philo interpreted the book in an allegorical fashion, giving a spiritual meaning especially to the detailed ritual requirements in its second half. Such a spiritual reading has survived in the Christian tradition, particularly in Holy Week and Easter, when many lectionaries set readings from Exodus alongside Gospel passages, and Easter hymns compare Jesus being raised from the dead with the deliverance of the people from Egypt.

> Come ye faithful, raise the strain / Of triumphant gladness
> Christ has brought his Israel / Into joy from sadness
> Freed from Pharaoh's bitter yoke / Jacob's sons and daughters
> Led them with unmoistened foot / Through the Red Sea waters.

This is rousing stuff, though sensitive Christian worshippers are liable to ask whether the picture of God described in some parts of the Exodus story is one which they can find acceptable. The deliberate hardening of Pharaoh's heart, the mass slaughter of apparently innocent Egyptians – these are serious matters which are too often ignored when the material is used in Christian worship, or indeed by Christians engaged in biblical study. In many respects later Jewish writers have shown greater sensitivity to these problems.

It may in part be for this reason that in recent years many other readings of the Exodus, both event and book, have been proposed. For some it is the great 'liberation' text, proclaiming God's power over the mighty of this world and his ability and willingness to rescue his followers from such forces. Feminist scholars have drawn attention to the significant role played by women in the story of deliverance, particularly in the early chapters. Thus in chs 1–2 vital roles are played by the midwives, Moses' mother and sister, and by Pharaoh's daughter. In 15. 20–21 Miriam leads the shout of triumph, though here the gloating over the defeated enemy brings out a less attractive theme. This raises the basic issue, whether modern readers, of any religious persuasion or none, can simply accept what is laid down in this ancient text as 'God's law'. This will certainly occupy us when we look at the Ten Commandments in ch. 20.

Alongside these concerns, which are mainly the product of our own age, more traditional interests continue: who wrote the book? Was the Exodus a historical event, and if so, when and where did it take place? Who was Moses, and how can we assess his achievement? These are some of the issues which the commentator on Exodus has to try to take into account, though it can be said at the outset that questions of this kind will play only a marginal part in this commentary. Two brief reasons may be mentioned: first, a degree of scepticism as to whether historical and geographical questions of this kind can be answered with the evidence available to us; and secondly, a conviction that the purposes of the Book of Exodus are not primarily of this kind.

In any case there is another matter which is at the literary level even more basic. When we read Exodus, are we reading a book which is complete in itself, or should we see it as part of a larger whole?

The literary setting of Exodus

The first five books of the Bible have traditionally been known as the 'Books of Moses'. The claim that he was their author is not found in the biblical text itself (and indeed Deuteronomy ends by relating the death of Moses) but that has often been understood to be implied. In any case a close connection between the different constituents is clearly envisaged. The name 'Pentateuch', commonly applied to the books Genesis–Deuteronomy, means 'Five Books' or 'Scrolls', and in all religious traditions which honour these texts they are commonly regarded as a unified collection. Among English Bibles it is interesting to note that AV/RV and RSV all had reference in their titles to the five books of Moses, whereas NEB/REB (and now also NRSV) call our book 'Exodus', without any indication that it is part of a larger whole. We shall briefly consider the question of authorship further on in this Introduction, but it may first of all be useful to notice the larger context in which the Book of Exodus is placed.

When we look at the text itself it is not wholly clear whether we are meant to see Exodus as a new start, or as making sense only if we are already familiar with Genesis. The opening verses of Exodus, 1. 1–8, certainly seem to assume the latter. A character called 'Jacob' is introduced without explanation. Who was he? He is clearly not an Egyptian, so why should he and his sons have gone to Egypt? Why was one of them, Joseph, already in Egypt, and why should Pharaoh have known him? It seems as if we need to know the answers to, or at least be able to make sense of, questions like this if we are going to understand Exodus. There are also occasional later indications that this is a continuing story, not a new one: 2. 24, and a few later passages, make reference to a 'covenant with Abraham, Isaac and Jacob' which is clearly at least an important preliminary to the story. Similarly in 6. 2–8 God reveals his name to Moses and indicates that this is a fuller revelation than the one already given to the ancestors.

Despite a few exceptions like this, however, impressions mostly change after the first eight verses. Much of Exodus reads like a new beginning. In chapter 3, for example, there is another story of God's self-revelation. In terms of new beginning this is ambiguous. Part of the story seems to be told as if it is a new God, previously unknown, who is now revealing himself; part of it, on the other hand, is very insistent on reassuring Moses that this God is indeed the God of their ancestors. Indeed, in the New Testament, Jesus is pictured as using this continuity as a clinching point in his argument with the

Sadducees. 'Have you not read in the book of Moses, in the story of the burning bush, how God spoke to him and said, "I am the God of Abraham, the God of Isaac, the God of Jacob"? He is not God of the dead but of the living' (Mark 12. 26–27). Not many people nowadays will find this type of argument convincing, but it clearly presents Jesus as regarding Exodus as part of a larger whole. But if that is so, it is very unexpected that Moses should be worried that his followers would not know the name of the God whom their ancestors had worshipped (and whom, incidentally, they had frequently addressed by name in the Genesis stories) (Ex. 3. 13).

Chapter 3 offers us another curiosity. God promises to take his worshippers away from Egypt to a 'land flowing with milk and honey . . . the land of the Canaanites (and other peoples)' (3. 17). But there is no suggestion that this is where they or their ancestors have already been! According to the Book of Genesis, this is the land which had already been promised to Abraham. We remember in particular the very solemn promise in Gen. 13. 15: 'all the land you see I shall give to you and to your descendants for ever'. Yet of that there is no mention in Exodus. It is pictured as a distant land, beyond the wilderness; there is no sense of 'going back home again'. So there is no easy answer to this question: Is it a continuation or a new start? It has features of both.

Comparable issues arise as we look at the end of the book. In one sense the story is complete with the building of the tabernacle in accordance with God's instructions. In one way that is an appropriate conclusion. As will be suggested in the commentary at that point, the links between Gen. 1–2 and Ex. 39–40 seem to imply that the building of the tabernacle was consciously expressed in terms reminiscent of the creation story in Gen. 1. 1–2. 3. The tabernacle was a newly created world in little. Yet in another sense it seems to be a curious place at which to end; once the tabernacle is built, what use is to be made of it? We may well feel that some such continuation as that provided by Leviticus is an essential follow-up to the Book of Exodus. And in a larger sense, of course, the Israelites are still in the middle of their journey to the 'land flowing with milk and honey'. Only with Numbers and Deuteronomy, the last books of the Pentateuch, is there any indication of impending arrival, and one has to go beyond the Pentateuch itself for that arrival to be complete, with Joshua's conquest of the land. All we can say is that we may in some senses regard Exodus as complete in itself, but that in other ways it will only make sense as part of a much larger story.

Source criticism

One answer to the kind of problem just rehearsed has been to engage in an analysis of the Pentateuch which divides it into different sources. The classic proposal along these lines, associated with the great German scholar Julius Wellhausen, and developed in its main outlines more than a century ago, has been to discern four such sources running through the Pentateuch. Two of them are primarily narratives; they have come to be known as 'J' and 'E', in accordance with the way in which they refer to God in Genesis. Sometimes God is referred to by the proper name Yahweh (German: Jahveh); sometimes the more general name for the divine, Elohim, is used. Source critics have felt that this usage was sufficiently consistent to provide a basis for division of the material.

The other two sources in this analysis are known as D and P. D stands for Deuteronomist, and is of course largely confined to the Book of Deuteronomy, though source critics have been sharply divided on the question whether it is possible to find significant traces of Deuteronomistic editing in Exodus. However that may be, all who have accepted source-critical methods would agree on the prominence of P in Exodus. P stands for Priestly, and it is regarded as specially concerned with genealogies and with the proper organization of the community's worship. On these grounds there has been very widespread agreement that the genealogies in 6. 14–27 and the detailed liturgical requirements in chs 25–31 and 35–40 are P material. Whether some of the plague stories in chs 8–11 are P has been more disputed, and there is also disagreement whether it is proper to regard P as a separate source or as the redactor and editor of the other sources.

This kind of source-critical analysis was long regarded as fundamental to the study of Exodus. In recent years, however, it has come under increasing criticism from a variety of directions. Conservative scholars have always rejected it, as running contrary to their belief concerning divine inspiration and, as a somewhat illogical rider to that belief, Mosaic authorship. Many others who are far from conservative have now joined in the attack.

Among those who accept source-critical principles there are those who doubt the existence of E as a separate source; the main criterion for identifying it – a distinctive way of referring to God – is in any case no longer applicable after Exodus 3, and there is no agreement that particular parts of Exodus can be attributed to E. (It is instructive to look at the widely differing attributions suggested by those treatments of the book which do accept four sources; undoubtedly the four-source theory works much better in Genesis than in the remainder of the Pentateuch.)

A further difficulty for source criticism arises from the fact already noted, that much of Exodus reads like a new beginning. This is unexpected if we are to think of it as composed of sources. It has led to a modified source-critical approach, which maintains that the sources underlying the final form of the book are largely independent of one another: blocks of material dealing with particular stages of the people's story rather than a continuous interweaving of distinct threads extending through the whole Pentateuch. But this is now so far from source criticism as traditionally practised that it has in effect become a different approach. Perhaps it would be more appropriate to regard the Pentateuch as a deliberately constructed piece of work, put together centuries after the events it described and making use of a variety of earlier material, the details of which are largely untraceable.

Such a view has something in common with the traditional understanding of authorship – that Exodus was deliberately brought together by an individual or a small group. But whereas the older traditions maintained that the reference to 'books of Moses' implied that Moses was the author, the understanding just outlined envisages the book being brought together at a much later date, perhaps during the time of the exile or the Second Temple period, that is in around the sixth or fifth century BCE, rather than in the thirteenth century or even earlier, as traditionally held. We shall in the commentary touch on the way in which Moses is presented, and ask whether anything may be known of him as an historical individual. All that need be said here is that a great deal of the book makes best sense in the context of an established agricultural community looking back from a distance upon its own religious traditions. Mosaic authorship can only seriously be envisaged if a substantial package of other presuppositions concerning the unique character of scripture is also accepted. That is too large an issue to engage in here.

It is striking that most recent studies of Exodus have paid little attention to authorship. Again, partly because of the feeling of many scholars that the questions raised by source criticism are too often unanswerable (and perhaps not of great interest when they are answered!), interests in that area have also largely moved elsewhere. What we have is the Book of Exodus in its final form; that is the departure point for many recent approaches to Exodus. Two in particular may briefly be mentioned here.

Canonical and liberation readings

Whatever else may be said about Exodus, it is revered as scripture by the Jewish and Christian communities. If this were not so, it is virtually impossible that we should have access to it, and the traditions it contains; it is only because of the reverence felt for the contents of Exodus as offering a divine message to religious communities through successive generations that it has been handed down. One recent approach to the book, therefore, has been labelled 'canonical criticism' (though this is a description rejected by some at least of those who approach it in this way). In such a view the most important thing to be said about Exodus is that it is scripture, and that it should therefore be explored first and foremost in that context. Whatever its origin, it was within the context of a religious community that the Book of Exodus was handed down. As we have seen already Jesus could refer to 'the book of Moses', knowing that the Sadducees with whom he was debating would recognize it as an authority within the religious tradition to which they belonged. Similarly, the interest in canonical criticism has largely arisen among those who are themselves Christians, and so the 'canon' of which they speak is the whole Christian Bible. It is important in this reading, therefore, to hold together not only the various references and allusions to Exodus found elsewhere in the Old Testament (and here clearly that description rather than 'Hebrew Bible' is appropriate,) but also the New Testament use of its themes.

It has also for the most part been within a church context that a second new approach has developed. The basic theme of Exodus is seen to be God's deliverance of his people from an oppressive tyranny. They are liberated to serve him in a new land. This theme of liberation has been much developed, particularly in Latin America, but also in other countries of the Two-Thirds World, as a way of understanding the true nature of God. When he is described as a saving God, that should not be limited to an idea of saving his followers from religious burdens and offering forgiveness of sins; it means, much more basically, that God is to be seen as a liberator from cruel and oppressive political regimes. These are valuable insights, though it is important also to recognize that they are themselves very selective. For a start, God's own behaviour is often presented in terms which some would describe as cruel and oppressive. The fate handed out to Pharaoh and many Egyptians, and that held in prospect for the inhabitants of the 'land flowing with milk and honey' is not a pleasant one. Even among the community delivered from Egypt, it is assumed that slavery will continue (21. 2), and of course the subservient position of women is taken for granted in the greater part of the book. As was noted above, women play a very important part in some of the narrative episodes, but in the religious and community laws of the second half of the book they are either ignored altogether or left in a very secondary position.

It will be seen from the above sketch that the Book of Exodus means many different things to different readers. It seems appropriate to end this introduction by setting out some of the assumptions that will underlie this commentary. First, we shall not attempt detailed source analysis, for the reasons set out above. Too often the answers provided by source analysis are to questions which no one would have dreamt of asking. Our primary concern will be with the book as a whole, as it has come down to us.

Our task here is made a little easier by the fact that there are no major differences in the various ancient forms of the book which have survived. In addition to the Hebrew (Masoretic) text, we have a different Hebrew text handed down by the Samaritan community and claimed by them to date back almost to the time of Moses. This 'Samaritan Pentateuch' is in fact of mediaeval origin, and differs only in details, a few of which are noted in the commentary, from the main Hebrew tradition. The Greek text, the Septuagint, at times offers slightly differing readings from those of the Hebrew, but these are rarely serious enough to raise major problems. Text critical problems do arise from time to time, but for the most part we shall need to refer to them only in passing. Reference must be made to larger commentaries for fuller analysis of the text.

Secondly, the historical and geographical questions which have dominated much study of Exodus will not be treated in detail here. As far as the Egyptian setting is concerned there is only one verse (1. 11) which seems to offer specific information, and as we shall see in our commentary on that verse the help that it appears to offer is largely illusory. No Egyptian ruler is named in the book; no cross-references to other events in the Ancient Near East are provided; no archaeological or literary evidence has emerged to enable us to place the

Exodus in a larger setting. To be blunt, it seems virtually impossible that there ever was a community which can be described as 'Israel' who were first living in and were then delivered from Egypt. The story must be allowed to wield its own power rather than be linked to a particular historical or geographical setting.

This approach has important consequences for contemporary readers. Doubts concerning historical and geographical matters may raise anxieties for some readers, and they are liable to be reinforced when they discover within this commentary a questioning attitude towards some of the laws and other requirements of the book. This commentary is written in the conviction that it is extremely valuable to read Exodus and other scriptural texts, but also in the conviction that these texts cannot simply be read off and applied to those who live in the third millennium CE. The Book of Exodus was written as an expression, no doubt an imperfect one, of a community's beliefs about God and their own status, perhaps some 2,500 years ago. In many ways modern society and modern humanity has made progress since then; in other respects regress seems more obvious. Here is one community's story; let us see where it leads us.

FOR FURTHER READING

W. Johnstone, *Exodus* (Old Testament Guides), Sheffield: JSOT Press 1990 is probably the best introductory guide to the main issues raised by the book.

Among commentaries the following may be noted:
B.S. Childs, *Exodus* (Old Testament Library), London: SCM Press 1974 (probably the best available large-scale commentary in English. Childs is well-known for his advocacy of a 'canonical reading').
J.I. Durham, *Exodus* (Word Biblical Commentary), Waco, Texas: Word Publishing 1987 (another full-scale commentary, which gives close attention to the Hebrew text, but is fully accessible to those relying on English translation).
U. Cassuto, *A Commentary on the Book of Exodus* (ET by I. Abrahams), Jerusalem: Magnes Press 1967 (a commentary by a Jewish scholar; extremely conservative on historical and geographical matters, but valuable for its literary insights).
S.R. Driver, *The Book of Exodus* (Cambridge Bible for Schools and Colleges), Cambridge University Press 1911. (Despite its age this commentary remains unrivalled for the amount of detailed information it provides in quite small compass. The thought of a work like this being offered to 'schools and colleges' nowadays is mind-boggling!)
G. Larsson, *Bound for Freedom: The Book of Exodus in Jewish and Christian Traditions*, Peabody, Mass.: Hendrickson 1999, appeared too late to be used in the preparation of this commentary, but readers may find its comparison of Jewish and Christian readings of Exodus offers some unexpected insights.

Not a commentary, but probably the most developed view of Exodus from the traditional historical-critical standpoint is that of M. Noth, *A History of Pentateuchal Traditions*, Chico: Scholars Press 1981 (translation by B.W. Anderson of *Überlieferungsgeschichte des Pentateuch*, 1948).

For those who wish to know more of different scholarly approaches to the whole Pentateuch, the standard introduction to the study of the Pentateuch in recent years is E.W. Nicholson, *The Pentateuch in the Twentieth Century*, Oxford: Clarendon Press 1998.

The following deal with particular parts of the book, or particular themes raised within it:

Different understandings of the role of Moses are presented by G.W. Coats, *Moses: Heroic Man, Man of God* (JSOT SS 87), Sheffield Academic Press 1988, and by J. van Seters, *The Life of Moses*, Kampen: Kok Pharos 1994. (Readers should be aware of the fact that the title of van Seters' book might mislead; this is no 'biography' in the conventional sense.)

A more optimistic attempt at solving the geographical problems raised by Exodus than that offered in this commentary is that of G.I. Davies, *The Way of the Wilderness: A Geographical Study of the Wilderness Itineraries in the Old Testament* (SOTS Monograph Series, 5), Cambridge University Press 1979.

The 'legal' parts of the book are dealt with by D. Patrick, *Old Testament Law*, London: SCM Press 1986, and by A.C.J. Phillips, *Ancient Israel's Criminal Law*, Oxford: Blackwell 1970, who puts forward a different understanding of the function of the Decalogue from that proposed here. A valuable exploration of the similarities and differences between law in ancient Israel and in the surrounding cultures is H.J. Boecker, *Law and the Administration of Justice in the Old Testament and Ancient East*, London: SPCK 1980.

Chs 32–34 are the subject of a study by R.W.L. Moberly, *At the Mountain of God* (JSOT SS 22), Sheffield: JSOT Press 1983.

For those who wish to know more of the work of Bishop Colenso, the most accessible and entertaining source may well be O. Chadwick, *The Victorian Church, Part Two*, London: A. & C. Black 1972, later reprinted by SCM Press 1987. Some feel that Chadwick has been somewhat harsh on Colenso, and a more sympathetic portrayal is set out in J. Guy, *The Heretic: a Study of the Life of John William Colenso 1814–83*, University of Natal Press 1983.

COMMENTARY

The Israelites in Egypt
1. 1–12. 36

The Israelites oppressed
1. 1–1. 22

1. 1–5 It is not unusual for biblical books to start with lists of names (cf. I Chronicles, Matthew). What might seem to the modern reader to be tedious repetition will have been for those who read or heard these texts in antiquity an important assertion of their identity. They were themselves part of the tradition to which these lists of names made reference. It is striking that the traditional Hebrew title of our book is 'Sheᵉmoth', 'Names'.

The very first verse offers a warning against too unthinking a recourse to source criticism of the kind that has characterized much study of the Pentateuch. In Genesis the ancestor Jacob is given a new name, 'Israel'. This is described twice (Gen. 32. 28; 35. 10), and the usage has often been regarded as a valuable criterion for source analysis. Yet here we find both names used in one verse, which can hardly be divided into two sources! Here *Israel* is used as a reference-point for the whole community; *Jacob* is the appropriate name to give to the individual who was the father of the children who are about to be listed.

The order of the listing of the *sons of Israel* corresponds to that found in Gen. 35. 23–26, Joseph being of course omitted here. Israel had sons by four different women; his two wives, the sisters Leah and Rachel, and their 'slave-girls' Bilhah and Zilpah. The somewhat unusual domestic arrangements involved in this kind of mini-harem pass without any moralizing comment in the biblical text. Here the six sons of Leah are listed first; then the second of Rachel's two sons, Benjamin (his older brother Joseph being in Egypt already); then the two sons of Bilhah; and finally those of Zilpah.

The number *seventy* here, as often in the Hebrew Bible, seems to imply completeness, as was already the case in Gen. 46. 27. Stephen's speech in Acts (7. 14) with its reference to 'seventy-five' people, embodies a different tradition, arrived at by adding nine sons of Jacob to the 'sixty-six' descendants also referred to in Gen. 46. 26. That tradition is already found in the LXX of Exodus.

1. 6–14   The description of the passing away of one generation as an appropriate formula to introduce a new set of circumstances is found also in Judg. 2. 10. The setting of the scene is completed with a four-fold picture of the growth of the community. The four verbs used to describe it are effectively synonymous. We find here for the first time a tension which will run through much of Exodus. Sometimes the community is pictured as a few helpless victims of oppression; sometimes emphasis is placed on their large numbers, as if they comprised a whole nation. Each can be seen theologically as a way of bringing out God's saving power, both as being addressed to the small helpless remnant and as capable of working for a whole nation.

REB takes the start of the narrative as being at v. 6, but it seems more likely that the new section begins at v. 8. (Thus NRSV and other English versions.) The section, with the possible exception of v. 11, does not lend itself to historical enquiry; the *new king* is not named, and he is pictured in a very folkloristic way as talking *to his people*. Egyptian rulers were pictured as incarnations of the god for whom they were named and would certainly have done nothing so demeaning as talk to their people. The thought that the Israelites were *too many and too strong* for the whole of Egypt is again a folklore motif. We are already being invited to think of the Egyptian ruler as both wicked and stupid.

This impression is strengthened by the picture in v. 10, which is unfortunately obscured by REB. The last phrase, *and become masters of the country*, is best translated, as in NRSV 'and escape (lit: go up) from the land'. If they were to leave the land, one might have supposed that the problem would be solved! We shall find plenty of further examples of this caricature of the Pharaoh's thought in the early part of the book.

V. 11 provides the first reference to *taskmasters*, and they will be mentioned frequently in chs 1-5. Sometimes they appear to be Egyptians, with the task of ruling the foreign slaves; sometimes it seems as if they are appointed from among the Israelites themselves. But sociological analysis is inappropriate here; this is a dramatic picture drawn to show how harsh was the life of the community.

Most attention in this verse has focussed on the reference to *store*

4

cities, Pithom and Rameses. This is the only passage in the 'Egyptian' part of the book which might be taken to offer specific reference and thereby a potential answer to some of the geographical and historical questions that we might wish to raise. *Rameses* is often held to provide a link with the Nineteenth Dynasty, often called 'Ramessid' from the name of its founder, Rameses I (*c*. 1320 BCE). The long-lived Rameses II (possible dates 1304–1237) is then held to be the Pharaoh of the Exodus. This is the so-called 'short chronology' for dating the events described in Exodus. It goes against the apparent testimony of the Bible itself, for I Kings 6. 1 appears to imply a date for the Exodus in the fifteenth century BCE, but this short chronology has been widely held to fit better into the larger structure of Ancient Near Eastern history, and many of the older 'histories of Israel' have embodied it in their narrative, claiming that we can be confident that the Exodus took place during the thirteenth century BCE, and perhaps be even more specific within that period. If it were also possible to identify the site of these store cities, then a clearer picture of the geography of these chapters would also emerge.

The confidence in our ability to reconstruct the history and the geography of Exodus that was being expressed thirty or forty years ago has now largely disappeared. Certainly this verse is a weak foundation for any such confidence. We should remember that an area called 'Rameses' had already been mentioned in Gen. 47. 11, which goes against the supposition that the name here provides a clue to the time of the building of these 'cities'. If it were anachronistic or an editorial comment there, as has often been suggested, why should that not also be the explanation here? Further, at least six different sites have been proposed for these store cities, which, incidentally, play no significant part in the Exodus narrative, save that Rameses is mentioned as the departure point at 12. 37. Rather than treating it as a geographical or historical pointer, it seems more likely that we are being invited to see a link here with Joseph's advice to Pharaoh in Gen. 41. 25–36. Even when the Egyptians take prudent action they are only following advice given by an Israelite.

Vv. 12–14 simply reiterate the harsh treatment which the people experienced. In vv. 13–14 the Hebrew word translated *ruthless* is actually used twice in describing this treatment (the rather free REB translation obscures the point); the same rare word is used three times in Lev. 25. 43–53, in a series of solemn warnings to Israelites against mistreating their slaves. Our passage can be read as showing the Egyptians failed to show the humanity required by the Israelite law;

the Leviticus passage warns Israel not to descend to the level of the Egyptians. More worryingly for the modern reader, both passages seem to take the existence of slavery for granted.

1. 15–22   This is clearly a new section; much less clear is whether it is possible to engage in precise source-analysis in this section. An obvious possibility would be to suppose that one source referred to the ruler as 'Pharaoh', the other as 'king of Egypt', but it is very difficult to carry such an analysis through without further surgery being applied to the text, and it is noteworthy that the Samaritan text differs from the main Hebrew tradition at v. 18. Whoever that ruler was, he remains unnamed throughout, whereas the two midwives are named: Shiphrah and Puah. In this way convention is doubly defied. The most important figure in the people's world is insulted by being left nameless; the two women are given names, whereas women often have to go incognito in the Hebrew Bible. Women play an important part in these first two chapters of Exodus. Some modern scholars have hailed this as showing that the biblical authors were capable of going beyond the usual androcentricity of their culture; others have warned that the naming of women does not basically alter the male-centredness of the text.

It is not clear whether we are to picture Shiphrah and Puah as being themselves 'Hebrews'. This would be the natural reading of v. 15, but it would then be surprising that they also attended Egyptian women, according to the natural sense of v. 19. At a later period of history to describe someone as *godfearing* (as here in v. 17) implied a non-Israelite who was sympathetic to Israel and its god, but that hardly seems to be what is intended here. In any case nothing can be read from this story which will tell us about the gynaecological customs of ancient Egypt. For the story-teller the point is simply another way of showing the superiority of the Hebrew women, able so readily to bring children to birth.

More difficult to resolve is the use of the term *Hebrew*. In the book so far the people have been referred to as 'Israelites'. Once again we have the question whether source analysis is the proper key to resolving this usage, and once again any attempt along these lines runs into considerable problems. The term itself also raises difficulties. It is often supposed in an imprecise way that 'Hebrews' is used in the Bible as an alternative description to 'Israelites'. In fact the use of that mode of reference in the Hebrew Bible is very limited, and complications also arise from the fact that non-biblical texts refer in a variety of contexts to groups called 'Habiru' or 'Apiru'. Such a description is often applied to those on the fringes of settled society, who were often perceived as posing a threat to that society.

A little over a century ago a collection of letters sent from Canaan to Egypt, probably in the fourteenth-century BCE, was discovered at Tell el-Amarna in Egypt. Several of these letters make reference to 'Habiru'. Thus Abdiheba the governor of Jerusalem expresses anxiety about the depredations brought about by the Habiru (*DOTT*, 39–41). We might compare them with modern gypsies, also perceived as a threat to the settled structures of society. It should incidentally be made clear that it is most unlikely that 'Habiru' was an expression referring to a specific ethnic group, or that the Habiru of the Amarna letters are to be identified with the Israelites. The wide range of references to Habiru makes it much more likely that the term refers to a social group.

At v. 16 the exact meaning of Pharaoh's command is not clear. The expression *check as the child is delivered* is rendered in NRSV as 'see them on the birth-stool'. The Hebrew word elsewhere refers to the pair of stone wheels used by a potter (Jer. 18. 3). Here it may refer to stones used as a birth-stool, or possibly to female genitalia, or (as is implied by REB) the reference may be to the sex of the newly-born child. In any case the command seems to be a foolish one. If the numbers of the Hebrews were to be reduced, surely the girl-babies should have been killed?

The whole picture is full of folkloristic touches; we can scarcely suppose that an Egyptian Pharaoh, esteemed as the visible incarnation of the god for whom he was named, would have spent his time in conversation with midwives, whose social status was not an exalted one. The whole story uses the familiar theme, popular from pantomimes and the like, of the foolish tyrant being outwitted. REB may be right in supposing that the midwives were given *families* (v. 21), though it is more literally 'houses'. We may be intended to see them as prospering socially.

V. 22 serves as a link between the foregoing episode, in which the plan to have all baby boys killed at birth has been thwarted, and the story in 2. 1–10. Even though the boys escape the first plan, it is intended that they shall fall victim to this new scheme, of throwing them into the Nile.

Moses
2. 1–7. 7

2. 1–4   The next story reads like a new start, with a 'once upon a time' character. Unusually the *certain man* remains unnamed and plays no further part in the story, Later in the book (6. 20) the father of the baby of this marriage is named as Amram, but the present story has no interest in him. The phrase 'daughter of Levi' would most naturally be understood literally, but most modern versions, including REB, have translated it *a Levite woman*. She will play a further part in the story, but her immediate kindred are not a concern of the narrator. Unnamed here, at 6. 20 she is not only given a name (Jochebed) but unexpectedly described as her husband's aunt! Our present story moves in a very different world from that of the genealogies. This point is also illustrated by the fact that the birth of the child in v. 2 is described in a way which certainly seems to imply a first-born, whereas later in this story the child has a sister and in 6. 20 and elsewhere he has an older brother.

No unusual circumstances surround the birth of the child, but we are soon told that he was *a fine child* (AV here: 'goodly'). The reference may be to his appearance, but is probably a deliberately vague term. What is to be done for such a special baby?

By a brilliant parody he is indeed put in the Nile, just as the Pharaoh had ordered should be the fate of all male children born to the Hebrews. But he is not simply thrown into the water; he is put in a *tebah*. Here *rush basket* is surely an inadequate translation, for this word is found in only two contexts in the whole Hebrew Bible: the present one, and the 'ark' made by Noah to rescue himself and his family from the waters of the great flood (Gen. 6–9). We are surely intended to see a deliberate cross-reference; just as once the blameless Noah had been saved from the destructive power of water in an ark, so now this child would be saved from the destructive power of other hostile waters. In one striking way, however, this story differs from the earlier account of the making of an ark. In Gen. 6. 14–16 God gives Noah very precise details as to its construction; here the initiative appears to be entirely the woman's own. There is no direct divine intervention in this story.

The details relating to *pitch and tar* add a little local colour, though whether 'pitch' was ever used in Egypt remains doubtful; it was more characteristic of Mesopotamia. Perhaps more important is the placing of the basket *among the reeds*. The 'reeds' (*suph*) have further overtones of deliverance, for the water where the people were saved from Pharaoh's army was the 'sea of reeds' (*yam suph*; 13. 18; REB 'Red Sea').

In addition to these inner-biblical references it has long been noted that this story has parallels in other Ancient Near Eastern traditions. The theme of the hero exposed in infancy is a widespread one. The best-known example is the legend of Sargon of Akkad, said to have ruled in the mid-third millennium BCE. The story seems to have been a well-known one, for several copies have survived; its original date is quite uncertain. The most immediately relevant part runs:

My changeling mother conceived me, in secret she bore me,
She set me in a basket of rushes, with bitumen she sealed my lid.

The story in Exodus might be seen as a direct and deliberate adaptation of the Sargon legend, in which case it could be regarded as in part at least a legitimation story, emphasizing that from such humble origins great leaders could emerge. More probably we should see our account as making use of a common rags-to-riches motif, emphasizing God's capacity to save his servants in the most unpromising circumstances. In this way it can be seen to embody the larger story of the deliverance from Egypt.

In v. 4 a *sister* is introduced. Elsewhere (e.g. 15. 20) we shall find references to 'Miriam', described rather oddly there as the sister of Aaron. Here, by contrast, the sister is unnamed, and seems simply to function as a necessary character in the story. Someone will be needed to act as an intermediary as the story develops, and dramatic irony demands that that 'someone' be closely related to the baby. Indeed we may note that if this was indeed the baby's sister it is odd that she should be described at v. 8 as calling *the baby's mother*, for she would have been her own mother as well.

2. 5–10 This section begins with another folkloristic touch. It is difficult to take seriously in historical terms the idea of *Pharaoh's daughter* being in the habit of bathing in the Nile! Protocol and hygiene would be equally offended by such a thought. But it is an essential element in the development of the story, as is of course the detail that she chose to *bathe* just where the basket had been left. *She opened* the basket, just as Noah had opened that earlier ark (Gen. 8. 6). The expression seems curious here: surely the basket cannot have been sealed, for how would the baby have breathed? The Hebrew describing the encounter

is more dramatic than the rather prosaic REB *it was crying*. AV 'And behold! the babe wept' caught this sense of drama. Pharaoh's daughter *was moved with pity*; it is striking, not only that women play a prominent part in these early chapters of the book, but also that an Egyptian, a member of the hated Pharaoh's own household, can be described in such sympathetic terms. And this is not simply maternal instinct, which would have been aroused by the sight of any vulnerable baby; she recognizes that *this must be one of the Hebrew children*. The child's sister can apparently approach Pharaoh's daughter directly (again surely at odds with protocol), and propose to find a *wet-nurse*. They were a regular feature of upper-class households in the ancient world, and indeed much more recently. We know what the dénouement is bound to be, though it is no less effective for that: *the baby's mother* is summoned and reunited with her child. It is noteworthy that the sister is described in verse 8 as an *'almah* (REB simply has 'she'; NRSV 'the girl'). This is the word used in Isa. 7. 14 (REB 'a young woman'), understood by the Gospel of Matthew as a reference to a virgin. It is usually thought that the Hebrew word meant a young woman of marriageable age, but that scarcely seems to be what is envisaged here, and is certainly at odds with the Miriam tradition later in the book.

The 'rags-to-riches' theme is completed with the taking of the baby into the royal household. The Hebrew of v. 9 is obscure in detail, but the general sense is clear enough, and again there is an element of mockery of the Egyptians. In God's providence the outcome of their cruel intentions is that they are paying a woman to *nurse* her own child, the one who in due course will overthrow their evil plans.

In v. 10, the child, so far nameless, is given the name *Moses*. He has been *adopted* by Pharaoh's daughter, and so is pictured as a legitimate member of the Egyptian royal household. A few scholars have made much of this, and have elaborated some remarkable theories about Moses' background; some have suggested a link (or even an identification!) between Moses and the Egyptian Pharaoh Akhenaten, known for his religious reforms. We can see the beginnings of this interest in Moses' background in the New Testament; Acts 7. 22 has Moses 'trained in all the wisdom of the Egyptians, a powerful speaker and a man of action'. Our text knows nothing of this. In the remainder of this chapter Moses is treated as if he were an Egyptian (e.g. at v. 19); that pretence is abandoned in the remainder of the book.

The folkloristic character of much of the material so far raises the question of the historicity of Moses, about which some scholars have been very sceptical. We should be wary of claiming historical reliability for this or that detail, but either there was a figure named Moses who was linked in some way with Egypt, or the compiler of the story has given him a very plausible Egyptian-type name, though this latter view may seem over-subtle. The name has the same form as that found in many Egyptian names, usually there linked with the name of an Egyptian god: thus Ra-meses. The Egyptian root *msy*, 'to beget' is added to a divine name to claim that the one so named was in a special sense linked with that god. Whether or not the 'historical' Moses ever bore the name of an Egyptian god we cannot know; if he did it is scarcely likely that it would have been preserved in Israelite tradition. What must be regarded as historically very implausible is the precise form of the story in our verse, which seems to imply knowledge of Hebrew on the part of an Egyptian princess. The link with a Hebrew verb *mashah*, whose existence is uncertain but is said to mean 'to draw out' is very unlikely; it is popular folk-etymology, linked with the 'drawing out' of the baby from the water, and perhaps also with the theme of God 'drawing out' his people from Egypt in the Exodus.

2.11–15a   A new episode is introduced with the characteristic *'one day'*. It is linked with what precedes by using the same Hebrew word as that found in v. 10, but REB obscures the connection by translating 'when he was old enough' in v. 10 and *was grown up* here. Taken by itself this episode does not imply any connection between Moses and the Egyptian court. He apparently knows (?by instinct) who *his own kinsmen* were. They are identified as *Hebrews*, and Moses is regarded as one of them. The verb *strike* (*nakah*) is ambiguous, perhaps deliberately so. It may or may not mean the death of the one struck. Whether or not the Hebrew was killed, the Egyptian certainly was, whereas in v. 13 the 'striking' equally certainly does not lead to death. The episode is described in a way which we may feel is almost casual. Moses apparently simply went up to the man and killed him. Our text scarcely regards it as murder; it is as if it were simply a literary device to lead into the next episode.

We are still in the realms of folklore. Moses somehow knows, as it were by instinct, which of the two engaged in the quarrel was *in the wrong*. The use of judicial language is surely ironical; Moses indeed has no jurisdiction over his fellows as yet. So when he knows that his deed is public knowledge he is afraid. We are not told how it did come to be public knowledge: in v. 12 Moses had seen *no one about*, as the curiously colloquial REB translation expresses it. By the end of the story we have quite forgotten that Moses is a member of Pharaoh's own household; he is simply regarded as one of the Hebrew workmen who had murdered an Egyptian. In the domestic scale of this whole episode, Pharaoh himself takes responsibility for punishing murderers. So, with another very frequent folklore motif, the hero must flee for his life.

He goes to the land of *Midian*. REB avoids a difficulty here by omitting 'the land of', which is in the Hebrew text. The problem is that there is no definable 'land of Midian', for the Midianites appear to have been nomads with no fixed area which could be described as their 'land'. The episode ends with one of the verbal repetitions which our author delights in. We have seen his repeated use of the verb 'strike' in different senses; now we have another verb used twice in this verse, translated first *settled* and then *sat*.

2. 15b–22   A very familiar scene, of the kind sometimes described as a 'type scene', is here played out. The hero is by a well; one or more young women come to the well to draw water; and the ensuing actions or conversations lead to dramatic developments. The well is an obvious symbol of fertility; one of those whom Moses assists will become his wife, just as in Genesis we have the courting of Rebekah ('Rebecca' in REB) (ch. 24) and of Rachel (ch. 29). Elements of the same pattern are found in the New Testament, in Jesus' encounter with the Samaritan woman (John 4), though there the author has deliberately transformed some of the familiar themes in the story.

It is not clear why *seven daughters* should be introduced. Seven is often a symbolic number but it is not easy to see what is symbolized here; only one plays any part in the subsequent story. In the Genesis examples of this type-scene attention is directed to one woman (Rebekah and Rachel each play an important part in subsequent developments). Here the daughter whom the hero will marry is not even named at this stage. *Troughs* play an important part in Jacob's courtship of Rachel, but only at the point where he tricks his father-in-law Laban, so that the linkage here may be coincidental. The hostile *shepherds* are however a characteristic feature of stories of this kind, providing an opportunity for the hero to display his bravery. We can be confident that this will lead to marriage between the valiant hero and one of the young women whom he has rescued. In the Genesis stories that happy ending is facilitated by the 'discovery' that the young man (or his representative) and the woman are related (Isaac and Rebekah; Jacob and Leah/Rachel). Moses is of course not pictured as related to the *priest of Midian*; it is his courage in driving away the hostile shepherds that commends him. The implication of vv. 17–19 is that the shepherds regularly came and harassed the women, but it seems simply to have been regarded as a fact of life; until Moses came no one had ever done anything to prevent it. Another mark in Moses' favour! One last characteristic of this type of story is found at v. 20, where the visitor is left outside while the necessary explanations take place (cf. Gen. 24. 29–30).

The priest of Midian is now named: *Reuel*. This name causes problems, for in 3. 1 he will be given the name 'Jethro'. The Septuagint Greek translation is even more confusing for it has the name 'Jothor' (its form of Jethro) in vv. 16–17 and Reuel at this verse. It has been surmised that Reuel was a clan name, and Jethro a proper name, but there is no evidence to support that. It seems as if the final author of the book was less concerned to reconcile divergent traditions than modern editors would be.

The story reaches its expected conclusion in vv. 21–22. The fugitive Moses stays with his new-found friends; his host's daughter is given to him in marriage; and a child is born. It is all told very matter-of-factly; there is nothing here comparable to Jacob's protracted wooing of Rachel. Indeed, with the important exception of the strange episode at 4. 24–26 *Zipporah* does not play a prominent part in the story, and in Numbers 12. 1 it appears as if Moses is married to a different woman. Here is a contrast with the Genesis stories. In them, Rebekah and Rachel remained as leading characters. Perhaps it is not surprising that they have remained popular as personal names today, whereas few baby girls nowadays are called 'Zipporah'.

The child that is born is here called *Gershom*. The form of the name varies. This is the only occurrence of this form in the Pentateuch; elsewhere (e.g. Gen. 46. 11) we find 'Gershon', used of what appears to be the same character. The Gershonites or Gershomites were a well-established branch of the Levites, and it seems as if the name is introduced here to link that group with Moses. It also provides opportunity for the kind of etymological fancy often found in the Old Testament. Whereas usually mothers named their children, here Moses himself gives the name, as its 'meaning' is only appropriate for him: *I have become an alien* (Heb. *ger*). It may be that a link with the verb *garash*, found in v. 17 ('drove them away') is also in mind here. Scientific criteria cannot be applied to this kind of punning etymology.

13

2. 23–25   The double spacing in REB rightly indicates that we have here a different tradition. Just as in the nativity stories in Matthew's Gospel the death of the first oppressor does not mean the end of anxiety, so here the death of *the king of Egypt* does not release the Israelites from their *slavery*. (The linkage with Matthew is not simply the use of a common motif; that Gospel would widely be seen as consciously modelling its story of Jesus' early life on Exodus.) Those who try to reconstruct a historical basis for our story may speculate on the identity of the 'oppression Pharaoh' and his successor the 'Exodus Pharaoh', but we have no evidence to back up such speculation.

Read literally these verses might give the impression that the *groaning* of the people was normally inaccessible to, or was ignored by, God. There are places in the Hebrew Bible where God seems to be presented unsympathetically, but this is not one of them. Rather the emphasis here seems to be to stress the link with the earlier part of the story: the *covenant* made with the patriarchs, *Abraham, Isaac, and Jacob*. We have seen already that there are few links between our story and Genesis; those that do exist, such as this, are usually ascribed to the literary source 'P'.

It seems as if something has gone wrong with the Hebrew text at the end of the chapter, which reads literally 'and God knew'. Either we should follow the Septuagint Greek and read 'he was made known to them' or understand that the Hebrew verb 'to know' has the unusual sense 'took thought'. This latter seems to be implied by REB, *took heed of it*.

3. 1–6   The theological, literary and other issues raised by Ex. 3 are so wide-ranging that whole books have been devoted to this chapter; we shall have to be more than usually selective. We may treat 2. 23–25 as a kind of interjection, giving the overall state of affairs. Now we return to *Moses*, and notice first of all that he has himself become a shepherd, in charge of the flocks of his *father-in-law*, here called *Jethro*. The phrase translated by REB as *along the west side of the wilderness* has been much discussed; NRSV 'beyond the wilderness' may catch the sense better, since a 'wilderness' would not normally be a place for pasturing sheep. In any case the sheep seem only to serve as a link with the preceding story; they are quite neglected in what follows.

Moses comes to *Horeb, the mountain of God*. Many scholars have taken this naming of the mountain as a later addition to the story. The difficulty is compounded because the 'holy mountain' at which God's self-revelation takes place is usually called 'Sinai'. We have no means of knowing whether Horeb and Sinai were alternative names for the same mountain; whether one was a range of mountains and the other an individual peak; or whether they were originally quite separate and only brought together by later tradition. Horeb is mentioned again in Exodus (17. 6), but that name is used in connection with the great events at the mountain described from ch. 19 on only once, and that very obliquely (33. 6). Otherwise only at 3. 12, with the requirement to worship God 'at this mountain' is such a link offered. It is difficult also to know whether we are to picture this mountain as already being known as 'the mountain of God', or whether that title is due to the dramatic events about to be described. Certainly if we are to take Exodus as it stands the latter seems more likely; no earlier traditions relating to such a mountain have been mentioned.

Source critics have commonly taken v. 2, with its reference to *the angel of the* LORD, as having a different origin from v. 1. But if we were to try to impose iron consistency as a criterion for source-analysis in this chapter we should be left with nothing more than a mass of tiny fragments. So there will be no further discussion of sources as we look at the story! We should, however, be prepared for 'angels' to play an important part in our book, for example at the crossing of the sea (14. 19), and as accompanying the people in their wilderness journey (e.g. 32. 34). The word effectively means 'messenger', that is, any divine emissary. Its usage here is quite different from that which developed in later Jewish and Christian tradition, and was beloved of Renaissance painters, of large winged creatures forming a kind of heavenly hierarchy.

More difficult to decide is whether botany has any part to play in our understanding. Much learning has been devoted to trying to identify some *bush* which could have appeared to burn without being consumed, but the effort seems to be misplaced. Apart from the fact that tricks of light can often lead to ocular illusions of this kind, the bush here is simply introduced as a means of alerting Moses to the fact that he should be on the lookout for something remarkable. It may be relevant also that the Hebrew name for the bush is *s\u1d49neh*, whose identity is unknown but may be a deliberate word play with 'Sinai'. At any rate Moses does make the appropriate response; and *the* LORD duly summons him in v. 4.

Preliminaries are not yet complete, however. What is to follow has the nature of a call-story, and a divine call needs the appropriate setting. It is instructive to compare this account with prophetic call-stories such as those in Isaiah 6 and Jeremiah 1. Just as Isaiah 'saw', so

Moses *turned aside to look* (same verb). This leads to a divine summons (cf. Jer. 1. 4–5), and the human response: *Here I am* (cf. Isa. 6. 9). Just as Isaiah's call most probably took place in the temple, so the place of this call is *holy ground*. The parallels with Isaiah and Jeremiah suggest prophetic status, but we may also detect priestly links here. The verb *come near* is very much a cultic verb. By far the greater number of its occurrences is to be found in Exodus, Leviticus and Numbers. It regularly relates to the priestly duties, so that by implication Moses seems here to be envisaged as the priest in the holy place. In such a setting it is still customary in many religious contexts, for example at a Muslim mosque, to *take off* one's *sandals*. There is a striking parallel to the phraseology here in Joshua 5. 15, where it looks as if Joshua is being deliberately portrayed as the true successor to Moses.

The *God of your father* theme will be important in the ensuing dialogue, and it is introduced here. When this passage is quoted in Acts 7. 32 the form is 'God of your fathers', and the Samaritan Pentateuch has that form here. Probably our text is right, but we should see the reference as being not just to Moses' own parent but to the ancestors who are then named. As we have seen there are not many references back to the Genesis story in Exodus, but ch. 3 offers important exceptions to that general pattern.

Moses hid his face. The idea of 'hiding the face' is most commonly attributed to God, particularly in the Psalms where many laments plead with God not to hide his face (e.g. Ps. 51. 9, where REB has 'turn away' for the more usual 'hide'). But it is also appropriate as a gesture of human inadequacy in the light of the divine presence; again we may compare Isa. 6. 5 and Jer. 1. 6 as expressions of human unworthiness.

3. 7-12   This section is of great importance if we are to read Exodus in terms of liberation theology. Whereas this chapter so far has focussed on God and Moses, now its concern extends to the suffering community. Previously they have avoided some of the worst consequences of oppression through their own efforts, but 2. 24 gave a hint that God would intervene. Now that is spelt out more fully. Not only are they to be rescued from *the power of the Egyptians*, they are to be given a land of their own. The rescuing is to be God's own action, though in v. 10 Moses' role is also stressed.

This is in effect the first passage in the book which looks forward, and the theme of 'entry into a promised land' will play a major role from now on. The way in which it is described is striking. If we follow the biblical account it was the same land as that from which Moses' ancestors, Jacob and his family, had come into Egypt. Yet as we noted in the Introduction there is here no hint of that; instead it is promised as a new land, not famine-ridden as had been Palestine in the time of Jacob, but *a fine broad land . . . flowing with milk and honey.* In terms of climate, this is an optimistic description, for much of the land is barren and subject to recurrent drought, but that is not the point of the presentation here; this is an idealized picture of an ideal land. Similarly, the solemn listing of the names of the existing occupants is a matter of rhetorical effect rather than a description of those who lived in Palestine at any particular period. *Canaanites* and *Amorites* are often regarded as different names for the same people, the native inhabitants of the area. There was a great *Hittite* empire which controlled much of Asia Minor in the fourteenth and thirteenth century, but most Hebrew Bible references to 'Hittites' have little to do with that empire; readers of Genesis would know that they occupied the land, for Abraham had purchased a burial-place for his wife from Ephron the Hittite (Gen. 23), and the point had been made that the chosen one, Jacob, must not marry a Hittite woman as his brother Esau had done (Gen. 27. 46–28. 1). The *Jebusites* were traditionally the pre-Davidic inhabitants of Jerusalem; nothing is known with certainty of *Perizzites* and *Hivites.* All of these will be the 'victims' of the liberation of Israel. In their fate no interest is here shown, though justification for that fate will be offered in Deuteronomy, especially ch. 7.

V. 9 in effect repeats v. 7, a fact which once would have been seized upon as pointing to different sources, but now seems better understood as a deliberate literary effect. That whole section may be seen as part of the calling of Moses; God's intention has been indicated, and now the servant is given his commissioning. Just as Jeremiah was to be 'a prophet to the nations', so Moses is to go *to Pharaoh* with a specific and rather daunting commission. As is usual in prophetic call-stories, this demand produces a protest: *Who am I?* Moses here is very like Isaiah acknowledging his uncleanness (Isa. 6. 5) and Jeremiah his immaturity (Jer. 1. 6). But as in those stories objections are overruled: God will be with the chosen messenger.

V. 12 introduces some new elements into the story. God's words '*I am with you*' prepare us for the self-revelation that is to follow, with its play on the verb 'to be'. Again, we have not heard previously about the requirement to *worship God here at this mountain.* Elsewhere the journey to the mountain is presented as if it were a detour from the

17

direct route to Palestine; here it is an integral element in the development of the people.

All this is presented as a 'sign' (REB: *proof*). It is not clear whether the sign is a reference back to the burning bush, or whether, as the REB translation implies, we should look forward: the act of deliverance is to be seen as the proof of God's power and willingness to act.

3. 13–15   These much-discussed[1] verses form the climax of this section. Taken literally, v. 13 might seem rather absurd, as if either Moses himself or the community have forgotten whom they worship. The author is introducing us to a theme which will recur later in Exodus and frequently in Numbers: the sceptical reaction of the people to all that is going on around them. In any case, the demand to know the name of the divine participant is a standard feature of theophanies; we may compare Jacob at Peniel (Gen. 32. 29) or Samson's father Manoah (Judg. 13. 17).

This last comparison is important when we come to v. 14. Many attempts have been made to find deep theological significance in this verse. The Greek translation led the way here, *ho ōn*, 'the existing one' inviting the envisaging of God in 'absolute being' terms. God as the 'One Who Is', or as the Creator 'who causes to be': themes like this have been prominent in theologies, with this verse being claimed as a biblical basis. But while the Hebrew certainly links the divine name with some form of the verb 'to be', it is improbable that such a deep significance should be read into it. A much more likely reading is to see here an element of the reaction found in the other theophanies, a refusal to let mere humans know the name and thereby too much of the character of God. The whole verse may well represent reflection on the well-known divine name Yahweh.

That divine name emerges in v. 15, which is joined very awkwardly to what precedes, and would follow v. 13 more naturally than it does v. 14. V. 6, as we saw, referred to 'the God of your father'; here we have '*God of their forefathers*' (Hebrew simply 'fathers'). This God is the source of Moses' authority. The verse ends with two statements which are in effect synonymous, set out in some versions (e.g. NRSV) as a poetic fragment. They are best understood as reflecting the way in which God's name was proclaimed in the context of worship. *Title* is a

---

[1] An article in a collection of essays published 25 years ago listed 74 other articles devoted specifically to these verses; they have also played a very prominent part in all 'theologies' of the Old Testament.

free translation of the Hebrew, which is traditionally rendered 'remembrance', but it brings out the underlying sense well. The phrase is very close to Ps. 135. 13.

3. 16–20 The implications of Moses' encounter with God are now spelt out. The facts that Moses has been away from his fellows in Egypt, and that his last encounter with them (2. 14) had not been a happy one, are set aside in the interests of the story. Now the Israelites are pictured as a religious group, led by *elders*, and the divine instructions are to be passed on to them. The verb *paqad*, used in a strong form to describe God's reaction to what has happened to the people, is difficult. REB *watched over* probably catches the sense. V. 17 re-iterates v. 8, but there follows a new implication. They are to request permission from the Pharaoh (again pictured as remarkably approachable) for a three-day religious pilgrimage *to offer sacrifice*. This motif, of a request for a brief absence in order to perform a religious observance, recurs from time to time in the next few chapters, but is in the end completely overlaid: not *a three days' journey*, but a permanent departure, is envisaged. It is not easy to know whether the lesser request is simply trickery, or whether some more ancient tradition underlies it. As set out here the former seems more likely; God foresees that Pharaoh will foolishly refuse them, and thereby bring upon himself greater punishments.

The last phrase of v. 19 is puzzling. Literally it reads 'allow you to go, not by a mighty hand'. References to a 'strong' or 'mighty' hand usually imply God's action. Presumably the point here is that God's mighty hand is indeed at work, but this time in a negative way, to thwart Pharaoh. God's *hand* is certainly pictured in v. 20, using a wordplay which cannot easily be reproduced in English. The same verb is used both of God (*'stretch out'*) and of Pharaoh (*'send'*). Pharaoh' s sending is totally dependent upon God's sending.

3. 21–22 A new theme is here introduced, one which has caused a good deal of embarrassment within the later Jewish and Christian traditions. It has entered English usage as 'spoiling the Egyptians'. The women of the community (men also in the Samaritan version) are to *ask* of their neighbours precious jewellery and clothing. The verb is ambiguous; either borrowing or permanent possession could be implied, though in the denouement the latter becomes the only possibility. It is curious that it is pictured that there would be Egyptian and Hebrew women living in the same house, since elsewhere the two

communities seem to be sharply divided, for example in the plague stories where Egyptians are affected and the Israelites are untouched. One traditional resolution of this problem was to suppose that the jewellery and clothing supplied the material necessary for the tabernacle in the wilderness, but that is scarcely compatible with the command to *put them on your sons and daughters*. Again the verb *plunder* makes it clear that this finery was to be regarded as spoils of war, gained through Yahweh's defeat of the Egyptians. We have to acknowledge the fact that our author, in his delight in telling the story of God's deliverance of the people, is quite willing to relish the deceit that they practised.

4. 1–5   Thus far it has been taken for granted that the community would recognize and accept the divine word. Now a new theme is introduced, which will recur constantly in the narrative parts of Exodus (and indeed Numbers). Two common verbs, here translated *believe* and *listen*, feature frequently in these episodes. Moses here envisages flat unbelief, just as in the prophetic call-stories the likelihood is that the prophetic message will be rejected (Isa. 6. 9–10; Ezek. 3. 16–21).

In Exodus and Numbers a regular way of showing how misplaced is any scepticism is the use of a sign from God. Characteristically the divine power is shown to be at work by the transformation of natural objects. We may properly see here anticipations both of the plague stories in chs 7–10 and of those stories in which the people complain about their lot (e.g. 17. 1–7). The sequence of events is stated in its most direct form here. The divine command is carried out; the resultant terror is overcome; and the result is that the human instrument is convinced. We noted in ch. 3 the use of the verb 'to send'; here it is found again – Moses is literally instructed to 'send his hand'. When we notice that that verb, *shalaḥ*, is combined with another identically-sounding verb, *shalak*, 'to stretch out' (REB: *throw*) we get some idea of the love of word-play displayed in these chapters. There are many more such examples, which can scarcely be set out in detail in a short commentary.

4. 6–9   Unusually two more signs are now provided without any response to the first one being recorded. *White as snow with disease* is REB's rendering of what other English versions have called 'leprosy'. The longer translation, though clumsy, is important, as the skin-disease referred to frequently in the Bible is certainly not true leprosy,

Hansen's disease. (Whatever it was, even clothing could suffer from it! [Lev. 13. 47–59.]) V. 8 reads very much like a conclusion, and it is unexpected to have yet a third sign added, as if by a kind of after-thought, in v. 9. It is very similar to the plague of blood described in 6. 14–25, and differs from the two earlier signs in that here there is no indication that the sign was actually performed: it was simply some-thing that Moses was to do in the event of disbelief, and the persua-sive power now seems to reside in Moses' own voice rather than in the signs themselves. This last point provides the link to the next episode.

4. 10–17 Similarities with prophetic call-stories continue. The inabil-ity to speak eloquently is a characteristic of those stories (Isa. 6. 5; Jer. 1. 6), and so the depiction of Moses as *slow and hesitant* should be seen as a literary device rather than as a clue to his character in trying to build up a 'historical Moses'. Later in the story he becomes very eloquent. Here he appears to be accusing God of doing only half a job: failing properly to equip him for the task in hand. That leads to a recitation of the divine origin of human powers of the kind often found in the Psalms (e.g. Ps. 94. 9).

At v.12 REB *I shall help you* misses an important word-play; a more literal rendering 'I will be with you' is needed to bring out the linkage with 3. 12. It is God, the divine name newly revealed, who will be with Moses. But Moses can offer only a very ambiguous reply: (literally) 'Send by whom you will send'. This might imply his willingness to go if forced to do so; more likely most modern translations are right in seeing it as a continuing demurral: *Send anyone else*.

God's irritation with Moses is predictable, but the proposed solu-tion is quite unexpected. We have heard nothing before of a *brother*. The account of Moses' birth in ch. 2 seemed clearly to imply that he was the first-born son of his parents, yet later (7. 7) Aaron is said to be older than Moses. 'Brother' can certainly be used of a more distant kinsman, but the later narrative of the Pentateuch seems clearly to imply that the two were full brothers. Again why should he be called *the Levite*? It can scarcely refer to his membership of a tribe or clan, for Moses himself would have belonged to the same group, and is indeed so described in 2. 1–2. The description must imply membership of some group exercising a priestly or oracular function. Nor is it made clear why Aaron should be *coming out to meet* Moses. We are not told where he is coming from, or why he should be *overjoyed* when meeting Moses.

The remainder of the section seems to have forgotten the divine anger; indeed Moses is, as it were 'promoted'. It reads very much as if this was the arrangement God had in mind all the time. But the way in which it is expressed is remarkable. The Hebrew taken literally says 'You (Moses) are to be to him for God'. It may be that a simple analogy is being drawn with the way in which prophetic messages were delivered, with Aaron as the (prophetic) speaker and Moses as the source of the messages, but it is very rare indeed in the Hebrew Bible for any human being to be described in such terms. The section is rounded off with a reference back to the *staff* – perhaps the one referred to in vv. 2–4, though v. 17 would read more naturally if we understood it as denoting a new gift from God to Moses.

4. 18   The last time we met Moses' father-in-law he had supposed Moses to be an Egyptian. No doubt he now knows differently. The Hebrew text here calls him 'Jether' but this is probably just a spelling variant which REB corrects to *Jethro*. The Midianite episode in Moses' life is now over.

4. 19–23   This verse is somewhat awkward in context: Moses' own wish being authenticated by a divine command. Readers of the New Testament will recognize how Matthew has neatly transformed v. 19. At Matt. 2. 20 Joseph and Mary are told to leave Egypt 'because those who threatened the child's life are dead'. Here Moses is to *go back to Egypt* for the same reason. All versions are agreed on the reference to *children*, though as yet we have been told only of the birth of one son, and v. 25 will refer to a single son. For the narrator these details are peripheral, and the narrative books in the Hebrew Bible often show such minor inconsistencies. More relevant for the moment is the *staff of God* which will enable Moses to carry out all the *portents*.

Two new motifs now emerge. First, the various signs had previously been performed to validate Moses' position in the eyes of the Israelites. Now Moses is to *display these before Pharaoh*. Secondly, we are introduced here for the first time to a theme which will be very prominent in the next few chapters: the hardening of Pharaoh's heart. It is God who will *make him obstinate*. This motif is an integral part of the story of the deliverance. Theologically, it is something of an embarrassing emphasis, for the Christian tradition in particular has been reluctant to picture God's activity in anything other than highly idealized ways. Not infrequently in the Hebrew Bible, however, the tradition pictures God as acting in strongly national terms, and delights in the people's enemies being discomfited.

This theme is now set out in terms which would be appropriate to a struggle between gods. They are seen as protectors of the families who served them, if necessary by resorting to war on their behalf. Israel's God is supreme and his *firstborn son* is secure; Pharaoh, portrayed by the Egyptians as divine, is incompetent and his son will be killed. The 'father/son' relationship became such a regular way of associating God and worshippers in later tradition that we may forget that it is rather unusual in the Hebrew Bible. Hosea 11. 1 is a well-known instance of the usage. It is noteworthy that the liberation here envisaged for Israel is that they shall be free to worship their God rather than to be given a new land.

4. 24–26 It is important, particularly for modern-day members of Jewish or Christian believing communities, to remember that we live in a world very different from that of the Bible. If a reminder is needed, it could be provided by this little episode, which has exercised scholars of all approaches for centuries. Indeed, the variety of translations offered by the ancient versions shows that it perplexed students in the ancient world as well. The problems it raises have led to all kinds of ingenious theories, but no 'solution'.

The first question we need to address is whether it should be seen as a continuation of what has preceded or as a new episode, distinct from what has gone before. In the first case, the reference in vv. 22–23 to *firstborn son* might prompt the idea that the concern here is with Moses' failure to have circumcised his firstborn son. If, on the other hand, we read this as a separate episode, we shall bear in mind that it contains no reference to this omission. Indeed the Hebrew text does not mention Moses at all in the episode. Where REB names him three times, the Hebrew text simply has 'him'.

Whoever is meant, *the LORD met* him. The verb often has threatening implications. We are reminded both of Jacob's experience at the River Jabbok in Gen. 32, also a life-threatening encounter with his God; and of the episode in Josh. 5. 3 where Joshua made 'knives of flint', the same word as is used here, and circumcised the people. The Hebrew text refers to 'feet', but REB is surely right in supposing this to be a euphemism for *genitals*. Less clear, as we have already seen, is whether we should interpret the 'his' as a reference to Moses. It would seem more natural to take it as a reference to the newly-circumcised son.

Moses is not mentioned by name in the Hebrew text: *Zipporah* is. A natural reading of this text would imply that she was required to perform some form of blood-ceremony which was considered to be necessary to appease an angry god. If that is so, then the episode remains unique; no convincing parallels have been adduced either in the Hebrew Bible itself or from elsewhere in the Ancient Near East. The expression put in her mouth is *'You are my blood-bridegroom'*. All manner of ingenious proposals have been put forward to explain this cryptic expression: some kind of puberty rite, taking the 'him' to be the son rather than Moses; an explanation of the practice of circumcision; a cult-practice held to ward off some wayside demon; even a legitimation of foreign marriages at a time when that practice was challenged. That is just a selection of the many proposals which have been put forward. All we can say is that it is a cry of triumph; the threat is warded off.

That becomes apparent in v. 26, but even here we are not sure whether *the LORD let Moses alone* is part of the original story, or an early explanatory comment. It is at least clear that circumcision is regarded as an important preparatory rite - in this case for the arrival of Moses in Egypt ready to carry out God's commission.

4. 27–31   This passage seems to know nothing of what has preceded. Whereas in v. 24 Moses was already *en route*, here Aaron goes all the way to *the mountain of God* to greet Moses. In any case the events described in the early part of the chapter are rehearsed, first to Aaron and then to *the elders of Israel*. Israel is here pictured as a small group, living together and easily accessible. Previously Moses had *performed the signs*; now Aaron does so. And the episode ends with the fears expressed in 4. 1 being shown, for the moment at least, to be groundless: *they were convinced*.

Some modern scholars have seen these early chapters of Exodus as the text for a series of religious ceremonies, and that would be supported by the end of this chapter. *'They bowed to the ground in worship'* (two verbs in Hebrew) is an expression normally used of some form of cultic ceremony. We know that the whole Exodus theme played a major part in later Jewish self-identification, but we have no specific evidence to support the idea of parts of our Book of Exodus being itself a cultic text.

However that may be, it is from this point on that we begin to notice a change in the character of the story. Much that has preceded might have led us to suppose that Moses was being groomed as a hero: the remarkable circumstances of his birth and up-bringing, his exile in an alien land, his commissioning by the god – all these, and other details also, are characteristic of hero legends from many cultures. Increasingly, however, once Moses has returned to Egypt, it is made clear that God is to be the central figure in the unfolding drama, with Moses and Aaron no more than instruments to carry out the divine instructions.

5. 1–5 *Moses and Aaron* are now back in Egypt, and this scene is the first of a series of encounters with the Pharaoh. The last time Moses had been in Egypt he had been condemned to death (2. 13), but this episode conveys no sense of their being under threat. Instead they address the Pharaoh as if they were messengers from God. The phrase rendered by REB as *these are the words of the* LORD is in fact the one that is frequently found in the prophetic books and traditionally rendered 'Thus saith the Lord'. It is often called the 'messenger formula'.

The message is that the people are to go to *keep a pilgrim-feast . . . in the wilderness*. This somewhat unexpected demand develops the point made by God to Moses at 3. 18, and as we saw there is somewhat at odds with the underlying theme, which is concerned with the total departure of the people. Were Moses and Aaron actually deceiving the Pharaoh? Such a suggestion may seem inappropriate for those who see in the Bible a model of ethical conduct, but it would follow the model set by some of the actions recorded of Jacob in Genesis. Stories in which the one who apparently held all the power was tricked are very congenial in this tradition.

In any case there is surely considerable irony in v. 2, where Pharaoh says *I do not acknowledge the* LORD. Though this translation is perfectly possible the point is really brought out more dramatically by the simpler rendering of NRSV 'I do not know the Lord'. The dramatic force of the next ten chapters of the book consists in Pharaoh coming to know the Lord and the kind of action of which he is capable. 7. 5, for example, may be seen as a deliberate reversal of this claim of ignorance.

The request is then developed. Older commentaries saw this as a parallel to v. 1 originating in a different source, noting that v. 1 has *the* LORD, *the God of Israel* and v. 3 has *the God of the Hebrews*, and that in v. 4 *the Egyptian king* is used rather than *Pharaoh*. But it is perhaps more likely that v. 3 simply develops the earlier request, bringing out a specific link with 3. 18. In any case we are now introduced to the theme of *pestilence or sword*, both of which will be very prominent in the next few chapters. With a nice dramatic irony they are first brought into the text as a threat to the Israelites; we know that it is Pharaoh and his people who will actually be the victims.

We are then taken back to a topic last directly described at 1. 14 – the harsh labour imposed upon the Israelites. If we were to read this story as straight history this would involve a very great lapse of time. Since the events of 1. 14 we have had the birth of Moses and his growth to manhood, his flight, marriage, the birth of children, as well as the death of the oppressor Pharaoh. But this material should be read as a dramatic presentation; the people are still at their *labours* (the same word as that translated 'forced labour' at 1. 11). The onerous nature of these tasks will be spelt out in the remainder of this chapter.

The reference in v. 5 is not very clear. The Hebrew text says that 'the people of the land were numerous', but this is a curious way to describe the Israelites. Nevertheless it is the sense accepted by REB, with its free rendering *your people*. NRSV, on the other hand, takes 'the people of the land' in its natural sense as referring to the Egyptians, by making a minor emendation of the Hebrew in line with the Samaritan version. Whichever is correct, the general sense is clear. It raises a question which recurs frequently in Exodus and again in Deuteronomy: the size of the community.

In some places the Israelites are pictured as very small in number. This is already spelt out at 1. 5, where the picture is of the members of one extended family. In the plague narratives the Israelites are pictured as a small group settled in one specific area of Egypt, and elsewhere also it is stressed that the community was a small one ('you were the smallest of all nations', Deut. 7. 7). At times, however, we are led to suppose that they constituted a very large group: this was implicit at 1. 9, and is spelt out at 12. 37, which refers to 600,000 males. It seems clear that different pictures are offered according to what seems appropriate in the context, and it would be unwise to take any one such picture as the more historically reliable. Sometimes, for example, the Exodus has been pictured as no more than the escape of a few slaves. That may be so, but we should not suppose that any of the pictures of numbers in the book offer a reliable support for such a view.

5. 6–14   This passage is unusual in containing no reference to Moses or Aaron. Some scholars have doubted whether the figure of Moses had anything to do with Egypt, and claim to find here traces of an early, non-Mosaic, source, but we may be sceptical as to the feasibility of such detailed source analysis. At the end of this section (v. 14) a

distinction will be made between the *slave-masters*, who are pictured as being Egyptians, and the *foremen*, who are themselves Israelites, but at the beginning they seem to be treated as identical groups. Even at v. 14 the Hebrew has 'the foremen of the Israelites', without any clear indication whether or not they were themselves Israelites.

In any case the community is pictured as under increasing pressure. This is the first indication we have been given of the details of the labour required. It is a feature of Hebrew narrative to introduce details of this kind as if they are already familiar, rather than spell out precise explanations. It scarcely seems feasible that *straw* could be turned into *bricks* with such speed as envisaged here; once again we have a dramatic device, a means of showing the increasingly desperate state to which the community was reduced. It is of course from this episode that the familiar English expression, making bricks without straw, derives.

At v. 8 the association of being *lazy* with the desire to *go and offer sacrifice to their god* offers an unusual juxtaposition. Presumably the point is to show how ignorant the Egyptians were of the exacting demands that Yahweh made of his people. But if that motif is unusual, the following verse offers a more familiar theme; oppressive regimes often suppose that keeping the subjects hard at work will leave those subjects no time or energy to think of anything else. The suggestion that the Israelites were lying when they requested time off for worship is an unexpected one, found only here and not developed in the narrative.

The picture in the last part of this section is a depressingly familiar one, with forced labourers being urged on to increasingly difficult tasks and being punished for failure. Some of the details, however, seem to owe much to dramatic effect. Thus, it is scarcely likely that the Israelites would have been allowed to *scatter all over Egypt* in their search for building materials. Nor is the difference between *stubble* and *straw* obvious!

5. 15–21 Not only Moses and Aaron, but even the *foremen* can have direct access to Pharaoh. Again dramatic impact takes precedence over historical plausibility. Indeed according to the Hebrew text they can even accuse Pharaoh of doing wrong to his own people (so NRSV); REB has made a slight modification of the text to achieve *the fault lies with your people*. The theme of laziness is re-emphasized, and the full tally of bricks required, and this leads to a theme not previously encountered: division within the Israelite community. The

word translated *meet* (v. 20) often has hostile implications, and so it is here. For no very obvious reason the foremen blame Moses and Aaron for their plight. At this point the theme of division will not be taken further, but it will recur again frequently when the community has left Egypt for its wilderness journey.

5. 22–6. 1   One of the differences between Jewish and Christian religious narratives is that in Christianity God is normally regarded as being beyond blame. It is, however, not unusual in Jewish literature, both biblical and post-biblical, for God to be blamed when things go wrong. Sometimes the impression is given that the human characters are wrong to speak in such a way (e.g. Adam in Gen. 3), but not infrequently no blame is laid at the door of the human being (Jeremiah's 'confessions' would be a classic example, e.g. Jer. 20. 7–12). So we should not be surprised when Moses passes on to God the criticism that has just been addressed to him. He is still resentful at being involved at all (*Why did you ever send me?*); he blames God for the mismatch between what he has promised and what he has actually achieved. He is being negligent in not taking proper care of his own people. God's reply alerts us to the fact that the real action of the book is just about to begin. The rather generalized translation of REB misses the irony in the divine words. Where REB has Pharaoh *compelled to let them go* and *forced to drive them from his country*, NRSV, translating more literally twice has the expression 'by a mighty hand'. This phrase, common in Deuteronomy of the Lord's own action, is here used of Pharaoh's action. But whereas God's power is effective, Pharaoh's use of a 'mighty hand' will lead directly to his own ill-fortune.

6. 2–8   Before the action begins, however, we have a further divine self-disclosure. In many ways this section can be seen as a parallel to ch. 3. In the days of classical source criticism this passage was attributed to P, whereas the earlier material was attributed to one of the narrative sources, J or E, or more often a combination of the two. Often, however, the impression was given that a careless final editor had simply failed to notice that he had left two duplicate accounts in the book. While we may properly see this as a P section, it should also be recognized that it has its own distinctive function within the book as a whole. In particular, whereas the story in ch. 3 had taken place in Midian, here it is in Egypt itself that God's power is displayed.

The self-disclosure begins with the announcement of the divine name: '*I am the* LORD (Yahweh)'. This phrase acts as a kind of refrain, occurring four times in the episode. While one must avoid rash generalizations about names having distinctive meanings, it does seem as if the point is to emphasize the effectiveness of Yahweh's power.

There follows a conscious link back to Genesis. As we have seen already, whereas the narrative material often seems to be unaware of the Genesis traditions, that link is clear and explicit in P. Here specific reference is made to Gen. 17. 1. There God had revealed himself to the newly-named Abraham as 'El Shaddai' (*God Almighty*), instead of the more general 'Elohim' (*God*) of Genesis 1. There is much dispute as to the significance of 'Shaddai'; feminist scholars have argued that it means 'breasts' and implies a female element in the divine. But the name plays no significant part in our story, which is concerned rather to show a further stage in the divine self-revelation; God's distinctive name Yahweh (*the* LORD) is disclosed.

Genesis 17 had also expressed the relation between God and people in terms of a covenant (v. 7). That theme is now developed, and the gift of *Canaan*, set out in ch. 3 as if it were a new possession, is here linked with the promise to Abraham. V. 4 of our passage picks up Gen. 17. 8. (REB does not make this link as clear as it might be; the word translated 'aliens' in Genesis is the same as that here rendered *foreigners*.) God's relations with his people are described as a series of covenants, of which God is *mindful* at each important new stage. The theme of the *groaning of the Israelites* provides a link with 2. 24: the action there promised is now about to take place.

The concluding part of this section (vv. 6–8) consists of a series of assurances, bound together, as we have already seen, by the repetition of the formula *I am the* LORD. We might describe the various verbs used as 'salvation words', except that salvation language has been 'taken over' in a rather different sense in the Christian tradition. They centre around the promise of deliverance from their present plight: *I shall free . . . deliver . . . rescue you*. We see here an obvious reason for the use of Exodus in liberation theology, and it was already being used in Psalms such as 136. 11–12. There follows the standard covenant formulary, with God taking Israel as his people and committing himself to be their God. Though there are many possible allusions to this formulary (e.g. the naming of the child 'Not my people' in Hosea 1. 9), it is most frequently found in prophetic texts usually dated from the exile or Second Temple period (e.g. Jer. 31. 33; Ezek. 36. 28), and this may give us a clue as to the dating of our passage. It represents the mature reflections of a later age on the way that God had once delivered the people from bondage.

Our passage ends with God's promise of the land through the renewal of the solemn divine oath (*swore with uplifted hand*). Whereas Abraham and the other patriarchs had been no more than sojourners, now the promise is of full *possession*. It is not difficult to see in passages like this one of the causes of present-day tensions concerning the possession of the land.

6. 9   What follows seems to be a terrible anti-climax. The people *would not listen to* Moses. This breakdown in communication is a theme which runs through the narrative parts of Exodus and Numbers. Elsewhere the people are strongly condemned for their failure; here the oppression they have experienced is put forward as an excuse. REB follows most versions in translating the last phrase as *depths of despair*, though elsewhere it means 'impatience' (Prov. 14. 29, 'quick temper'). In any case the theme here is used as a contrast to what is to follow in v. 12.

6. 10–13   God's instructions seem to Moses to be unreasonable. If his own people refused to listen, why should *Pharaoh* do so? This seems to be part of a justification of Moses. Instead of setting him in opposition to God, his very human limitations are emphasized. Those limitations are described in a curious idiom: where REB has *a halting speaker*, the Hebrew could be literally translated 'I am uncircumcised of lips'. This extraordinary usage is a metaphor which is quite common in exilic and later texts; as well as lips, references to circumcision could be applied to heart, ears, and even fruit-trees (Lev. 19. 23)! Presumably circumcision was regarded as so much a distinctive feature of God's community, being closely linked with its covenant status (Gen. 17. 9–14), that it could be used figuratively in this wide-ranging way. At any rate the divine commands are reiterated, with Moses' role concerning both his own people and *Pharaoh* laid down.

6. 14–27   We might have expected action; instead, we get an extended list of names. Here, as elsewhere in the Old Testament, the identity of the community is a matter of great importance, and genealogies such as this are important in establishing that identity. Genealogy was a creative art in the ancient world, and it would be unwise to treat this and similar lists as if they were objective records such as modern

censuses claim to be. This list functions in a way similar to that in Gen. 10, which introduced the story of Abraham.

It begins as if all the tribes are to be enumerated, and both the words translated *families* were originally social terms denoting 'clan' or the like. The traditions relating to *Reuben* all describe him as *Israel's eldest son* (Gen. 29. 32), but the tribe later became quite insignificant. (It is not possible in a commentary of this size to devote attention to the individuals named; the *Enoch* mentioned here is of course quite different from the figure of Gen. 5. 21–24 , around whom many later traditions developed.) *Simeon* was the second-born son of Leah to Jacob (Gen. 29. 33), but this group also descended into obscurity. Though conventionally one of the ten 'northern' tribes which separated from the South after the death of Solomon (I Kings 12), Simeon was actually a small southern group, very much subject to Judah. Thus far the list is virtually identical with that found in Gen. 46. 8–10, even down to the detail of the parentage of *Saul*, another figure who is not to be confused with a better-known namesake – in this case King Saul.

At v. 16, however, the form and thrust of the list change, and the expected roll of all the Israelites is never completed. From now on all the concern is with *the sons of Levi*, an important pointer to the later part of the book which is largely devoted to priestly matters. A formal introduction is offered, using the word *tol^edoth* (REB *seniority*), a word found frequently in Genesis to describe the different stages of the story. (REB understandably but regrettably uses different translations of the same Hebrew word, e.g. 'story' at Gen. 2. 4; 'account' at 37. 2.) Uniquely, the age of Levi is also recorded.

We might suppose that *Gershon*, listed here and elsewhere (Gen. 46. 11) is quite distinct from 'Gershom', Moses' son according to 2. 22. Later tradition, however, often confused the two. Though Gershon is described as the senior, fewer details are offered about him than about *Kohath*, the ancestor of Moses, whose age is recorded. The section seems to be completed at v. 19, the end of which balances out the beginning at 16a.

An additional table is however provided which spells out more precisely the place of *Aaron and Moses* among the Levites. It starts with what has been a continuing embarrassment for strict Jewish interpreters. *Amram*, the son of Kohath, had as wife *Jochebed*, and she is said to have been his aunt (*father's sister*), and it was from this incestuous relation, forbidden by Lev. 18. 12, that Aaron and Moses were born. Already as early as the Greek translation of the Hebrew Bible (*c.* third century BCE) this was a difficulty, resolved there by describing Jochebed as Amram's cousin.

The name 'Jochebed', found here and at Num. 26. 59 has another interest. Should we see the 'Jo-' prefix as an indication that she was a worshipper of Yahweh? It was a very widespread custom at a later period to give names containing a divine element; the suffix '-iah' is the most common such form, but 'Jo-' prefixes are also found, as for example in kings' names such as 'Joash'. It is certainly possible that Jochebed is a name that has been formed in this way, in which case we should have a different angle on how Moses came to be a devotee of Yahweh. This ties in with what is sometimes called 'the Kenite hypothesis', the proposal that the origins of Yahweh-worship are to be found among the Kenites, a group often mentioned favourably in the Hebrew Bible, and that Moses' father-in-law, and thus also his wife, had come to be worshippers of Yahweh. It is an ingenious theory, but depends on too many untestable hypotheses to be anything more.

We know little about those named in vv. 21–22, though there are allusions to several of them in what appear to have been inter-priestly conflicts. Thus *Korah* and his group are condemned in Num. 16, though the use of the name in the titles of Pss 42–49 suggests that they were accepted in some quarters; and *Mishael* and *Elzaphan* are mentioned in Lev. 10. 4, again in a context of inter-priestly rivalry. The right to the priestly office was a very contentious issue in Second Temple Judaism.

The family of *Aaron* is introduced in the same way as that of Amram. *Elisheba* is otherwise unknown but it is interesting to note that *Amminadab* and *Nahshon* feature in the genealogies of Jesus (Matt. 1. 4; Luke 3. 32–33), though there without the priestly links. The four sons of Aaron are frequently mentioned in genealogies; the priestly service of *Nadab and Abihu* is rejected in Lev. 10, but disputes between those claiming descent from *Eleazar* and *Ithamar* continued right down to the beginning of the Common Era. The *sons of Korah* listed here appear to be brothers; in I Chron. 6. 22–23 (MT 6. 6–7) they are listed as succeeding generations. These details are mentioned here to illustrate how easy it was for contradictions to emerge, either deliberately or accidentally, in lists of this kind. Of the remaining names we may simply note that *Phinehas* in v. 25 was to play an important (and appalling) part in the Book of Numbers (Num. 25. 7–11), a feat which was to earn him continuing recognition (Ps. 106. 30–31).

The genealogy is rounded off in a fashion which makes it clear that *Aaron* rather than *Moses* was the real centre of attention. The picture conveyed here of the Exodus itself is also a striking one: not a mere escape, but a formal departure of the people *mustered in their tribal hosts*. In this tradition, too, *Moses and Aaron told Pharaoh . . . to let the Israelites leave*. We have moved a long way from the slave labour of ch. 5.

6. 28–7. 7 This section largely recapitulates points already raised. Older commentators regarded such repetition as evidence of different sources; the modern fashion is to see this as a literary device, recalling readers and hearers to the main plot. In any case it is not simple repetition. Thus, when Moses again *protests* because he is *a halting speaker* there is now no condemnation of him. Rather he is to be as *god for Pharaoh*, with *Aaron as* his prophetic *spokesman*, a theme already touched upon at 4. 16. V. 3 makes it clear that it is Yahweh's own action which will harden Pharaoh's heart; that is not to be seen as a result of the plagues, but is already decreed. Pharaoh is in this picture simply reduced to a puppet-like condition. Indeed, the author takes the opportunity to put into God's mouth a strong assertion that he alone is the one who is responsible in military fashion for delivering the people .

V. 7 ends with another divine self-disclosure, *I am the* LORD, comparable to those we noted in 6. 2–8. Here, however, it is to the Egyptians that God will disclose himself, effectively negating Pharaoh's claim at 5. 2 not to know the Lord. The obedience of *Moses and Aaron* to God's commands is stressed, as is usual in the P material; only in the narrative sources are they sometimes linked with the people's scepticism.

The section ends with an unexpected note of the ages of *Moses* and *Aaron*. As far as Moses is concerned, this should probably be seen as a division of his life into three periods of forty years, from his birth in Egypt to his 'exile' in Midian, then in Egypt, and finally in the wilderness, so that he is said to have been 120 when he died (Deut. 34. 7). We need not take the figures literally; Moses' actions in Exodus are not those of an eighty-year-old. The tradition of Aaron being older than Moses is, as we have already noted, at odds with the account of Moses' birth in ch. 2.

The struggle with Pharaoh
7. 8–11. 10

7. 8–13   We now move forward to the next major theme: the plagues. We shall notice when we get to the very end of the book (see the notes on 39. 43–40. 1 below) that one way of looking at the whole theme of Exodus is as a new creation, relating specifically to the Israelite community. If that is so, it might be appropriate to understand the whole episode of the plagues, culminating in the death of the first-born in ch. 12, as a story of 'uncreation'. There has to be a purging out of hostile elements before a renewed creation can be set in motion. Certainly the whole sequence of plague stories shows Yahweh as being in control of natural phenomena as well as of historical events.

Some of the themes of the plague narratives have already been touched upon. In 4. 1–5 various signs had been carried out to persuade the Israelites that Moses' capacity came from God; now similar signs are to be demonstrated before Pharaoh and his servants. The role of Moses and Aaron is somewhat confusing. Whereas in v. 8 both are addressed together, in v. 9 Moses appears to be pictured as an intermediary, passing on instructions to Aaron. Perhaps this is what was meant by the depiction of their roles in 7. 1. As the plague stories develop sometimes Moses is the only intermediary, and sometimes Aaron is associated with him. No particular literary or theological implication seems to follow from this variety.

The initiative comes from Pharaoh, who is investigating their credentials (*demands some portent*). God tells them what to do, and they are described as doing it. The similarities with 4. 2–4 are obvious enough. One difference is that whereas in 4. 3 the staff became an ordinary snake, here it is transformed into a *tannin*, a word which may well have more mythological overtones. REB makes a distinction. It had translated 4. 3 with 'snake', whereas here we have *serpent*. It is clear that with its mysterious origins no ordinary creature is produced here.

At this point new characters are introduced into the story: *the wise men and the sorcerers*, described collectively as *the Egyptian magicians*. They have not previously appeared in Exodus, though they were mentioned in Genesis, where their inadequacy became Joseph's opportunity (Gen. 41. 8). Here for the moment it seems as if they are quite capable; they *did the same thing by their spells*. But this favourable impression is quickly modified; they lose their staffs, *swallowed up* by that of Aaron! Curiously, it is the staffs and not the serpents that do the swallowing. The section ends with a motif that will become more and more prominent in the next few chapters: *Pharaoh was obstinate . . . he would not listen*. There are no immediate consequences, but as the story unfolds the repercussions of such an attitude will be serious indeed.

7. 14–18   After this preliminary the nature of the first plague is described. Much attention has been devoted to the attempt to detect different sources underlying the plagues, and it may well be that the stories have a varied background. We shall not attempt here, however, to engage in precise source analysis. It is very doubtful whether such analysis can be carried out on a secure basis. The story begins with the same curious picture as we met in ch. 2, of the royal family bathing in the Nile. Moses (Aaron is not present in this episode) is to take with him the magic *staff*; it is not clear whether the reference is to v. 9, which would seem natural, except that the word here used for *snake* is that found in 4. 3. In any case, the earlier demand for the people to be released to hold a festival in the *wilderness* is repeated, with the warning that otherwise Pharaoh will come to know the hard way that *I am the* LORD. With brutal directness vv. 17b–18 describe the first plague.

7. 19–21   God's orders are now carried out, with Aaron now participating and a more elaborate description offered of their effect. The *rivers* referred to here and at 8. 5 are literally 'Niles', an indication that in Egypt there was in effect only one great river. REB follows most translations in understanding 'wood and stone' as referring to *wooden bowls and stone jars*, but it might be general, a reference to trees and stones to denote the total nature of the plague, or even an allusion to Egyptian gods. 'Wood and stone' in the Old Testament often refers to idols.

Various attempts have been made to provide a naturalistic explanation of what took place. It is claimed, for example, that the lower reaches of the Nile sometimes appear red because of excessive flooding of its feeder-waters, the Blue Nile and the Atbara, which bring down 'red earth'. One need not absolutely exclude this as a contributory element to the tradition, but that is not the real point of the story. For the story-teller this is *blood*, not just some natural phenomenon. Yahweh's power at work is emphasized in such details as the death of the fish and the stink of the river, neither of which would be caused by the 'red earth' phenomenon. Indeed by the end of the account the blood is not confined to the river: *there was blood everywhere in Egypt.*

7. 22–25   Commentators have been slow to see the – surely deliberate – comic aspects of this part of the story. By showing that they could do *the same thing* the *Egyptian magicians* were only making matters worse. We need not ask how they could have shown their skill if there was already blood everywhere. In any case *Pharaoh remained obstinate.* A touch of verismilitude is then offered by the account of the Egyptians seeking alternative water supplies and the note of the passage of time.

8. 1–4   (In the Hebrew text ch. 7 continues for another four verses; some commentaries follow the Hebrew verse numbering, so it is important when reading other books to check which system is being followed. Here we follow REB.) The threat of the second plague is now spelt out. *Frogs* are mentioned in the Hebrew Bible only with reference to the plague story, so we cannot be certain whether a particular kind of creature is intended. The statement that the *Nile will swarm with them* recalls Gen. 1, where the creation story has reference to 'swarming creatures' (1. 21, etc.). But a main point here again appears to be the comic effect brought out by the universal nuisance of frogs everywhere, even *clambering* over Pharaoh himself.

8. 5–7   These verses might be a repetition of the preceding from a different source, but they can certainly be read as a repetition for dramatic effect, with the *magicians'* efficacy in making matters worse.

8. 8–15   A new theme is now introduced: a request from *Pharaoh* to *Moses and Aaron* that they intercede for him. This is the first, as yet indirect, hint of a recognition by Pharaoh of Yahweh's supremacy. The exact force of Moses' reply is not at all clear, as is shown by the literal translation found in AV: 'Glory over me; when shall I intreat for thee . . .?' Many suggestions have been made, either to emend the text or to find in it some meaning such as 'cast lots' to decide the appropriate time. REB probably catches the sense with *I give your majesty the choice of a time*, with the implication that Yahweh can act at whatever time Pharaoh suggests. This is supported by *tomorrow* in v. 9, and the dramatic effect is increased by the repetition in v. 11 of what had already been spelt out in v. 9 to illustrate the scale of the problem.

VV. 13–14 utilize a motif common in folklore in tales such as that of the sorcerer's apprentice: a request carried out literally without proper thought of the consequences. So Pharaoh got what he asked for: *all the frogs perished.* What he had not thought of was the disposal of them. So they had to be *piled into countless heaps,* and, of course, *the land stank.* Perhaps this is a deliberate contrast to the picture of the 'fine broad land' promised to the Israelites. However that may be, the immediate effect of Pharaoh's *relief* – he was presumably not personally involved in clearing the piles of frogs – is that he *became obdurate.* But of course his renewed hardness of heart need be no cause for concern: it was *as the* LORD *had foretold.*

8. 16–19   Another plague follows. Its exact nature is uncertain: REB's *maggots* catches the unpleasantness of the visitation as well as anything. The equivalent modern Hebrew word means 'lice'. The important development here is that on this occasion *the magicians . . . failed* when they tried to emulate Moses and Aaron. We might suppose that it would have been difficult to discern this, if *the maggots were everywhere,* and that in any case the rest of the population would have been much relieved that the affliction was not even greater. But of course a theological point, common to stories of this kind, is being made: as in Daniel 2, and perhaps in the story of the magi in Matthew 2, we have here the theme of foreign magicians being forced to see God's power at work in a way that they could not emulate. But though the magicians recognized this, *Pharaoh* of course *remained obstinate.*

8. 20–29   This next plague looks very much like a variant of the preceding one, again featuring some unidentifiable parasitic insect: *swarms of flies* in REB. As in 7. 15 we have the odd picture of Pharaoh bathing in the Nile, and the basic demand for release which Moses is sure in advance will not be granted. But at v. 22 a new theme is introduced, which will play an important part in the remainder of the plague stories. An *exception* is to be made of *Goshen, the land where my people live.* Goshen had been frequently named in Gen. 46–47 as an appropriate place for the Israelites to settle, but this is its first mention in Exodus. We do not know where it may have been; the biblical writers clearly envisaged it as being in the eastern part of the Nile delta, but we cannot be certain whether it was a genuine Egyptian name or simply a biblical construct. There is no reference to the name in ancient Egyptian material.

English versions have differed in their understanding of v. 23.

Traditionally instead of REB *distinction*, which implies a modification of the Hebrew text, a reference to 'redemption' has been seen (see for example NRSV margin). But the ancient versions already made the change implied by REB, which is probably right here. In any case no elaborate theology of redemption is here implied. No reason is offered why the exception of Goshen was to be postponed until *tomorrow*.

At v. 24 a tension arises which will recur in the remaining plague stories. If the devastation brought about by each plague was so great, what was left to be affected by later plagues? The Hebrew text, followed by NRSV, seems to state that 'the land was ruined because of the flies'; REB avoids the problem by its translation, *was threatened with ruin*. In any case the damage is pictured as sufficiently great to wring a first concession from Pharaoh; the people may worship, *but in this country*.

This leads to a complicated exchange between Pharaoh and Moses. We are first introduced to the theme of Israelite practice as *an abomination to the Egyptians*. Like the reference to Goshen, this recalls Gen. 46–47, where the fact that the Israelites were shepherds was similarly described. (The same phrase is translated '[regarded as] unclean by Egyptians' by REB at Gen. 46. 34.) Such a sight would lead the Egyptians to *stone* (the Israelites) *to death*. In view of the story in Ex. 1–2 we might have supposed that Pharaoh would have welcomed such an outcome, but here clearly the potential loss of Israelite labour is the main concern. So the *three days' journey*, first mentioned at 3. 18, is revived, and Pharaoh in his response for once seems to behave very reasonably; they may go to *the wilderness* for their worship as they request, though *not very far* (!) and are asked to *intercede* for Pharaoh. Later Jewish tradition, beginning already at Jer. 15. 1, made much of Moses' power as intercessor. The reference to *tomorrow* rounds the section off neatly by a link back to v. 23. The verb translated *trifle* is uncertain; it probably has the sense of cheating, as in NRSV 'deal falsely'.

8. 30–32   Moses' intercession is of course successful. Equally predictable is Pharaoh's failure to honour his word. No reason is stated, but once again he *became obdurate*.

9. 1–7   By now the scenario is familiar. Pharaoh's obstinacy will bring about another plague, and it is threatened in words closely similar to 8. 1–2. This time, however, it is described in very general terms: *a devastating pestilence*, so universal in nature that all the Egyptian *livestock* is affected. The theme of a distinction between Egyptian and Israelite possessions, first mentioned at 8. 22, is now carried further, and is indeed the main point of this episode. *All the livestock of Egypt died, but from Israel's livestock not one single beast died.* Here more than anywhere we are in the realm of the dramatic story; it would be quite inappropriate in such a world to ask where Pharaoh obtained his horses to pursue after the fleeing Israelites in ch. 14, or even what herds remained to be brought to shelter in v. 19 of this chapter. For the moment we are simply given a picture of a Pharaoh who has taken leave of his senses. Despite discovering that among the Israelites *not an animal had died*, by contrast with his own people's devastating losses, he nevertheless *remained obstinate*. 'Let my people go', is the refrain of the song of liberation; as yet Pharaoh *would not let the people go*.

9. 8–12 After the very generalized description of the preceding section much more specific language is now used. There is no introduction as such, simply the divine command. At first the picture conjured up is – perhaps deliberately – comic. Normal court protocol does not involve standing in front of the ruler throwing around *soot* from a conveniently adjacent *kiln*. *The whole of Egypt* is affected, and the *festering boils* develop on *man and beast*. *All the Egyptians* suffered, presumably including Pharaoh himself, though the text makes nothing of this. The *magicians* return, and again we see the cruelly comic effect; they *were no match for Moses*, because they were themselves suffering from *the boils*. This little episode, perhaps more than any of the other plague stories, brings out the glee of the oppressed at the suffering of their oppressors. (The boils, incidentally, are the same as the affliction of Job, though REB there describes them as 'running sores', Job 2. 7.)

9. 13–21 Deliberate repetition, to build up the sense of drama, is a feature of the plague stories, and v. 13 follows 8. 20 and 9. 1 very closely. But there is also variation, and vv. 14–16 bring out certain explanatory features not found elsewhere. Moses is to convey a message directly from Yahweh to Pharaoh. It is stressed that it is from Yahweh himself that the plagues come, and that they have a purpose: *that you may know that there is none like me in all the world*. Here, as in 7. 3 but rarely elsewhere, the plagues are treated as a conscious series, deliberately organized. REB *against you yourself* misses the point of

the Hebrew, which is 'against your heart', with a surely deliberate allusion to the way in which Pharaoh constantly 'hardened his heart'. (The heart, here as often in the Hebrew Bible, is the seat not of emotion but of decision; we might almost understand it as 'mind'.)

Somewhat ironically Pharaoh is then reminded how fortunate he is; had Yahweh showed the power of which he was capable, Pharaoh (and presumably his people) *would have vanished from the earth*. But they have been spared, in order that the *fame* of Yahweh might be the more widely recognized. It is not specified who is to *spread* (God's) *fame all over the world*.

Vv. 14–16 function as an extended introduction to the next plague: *a violent hailstorm*, brought about because of Pharaoh's obstruction. Presumably his arrogance is meant. The storm is characterized in a way common to stories of this kind – it is the worst such phenomenon ever known. Hail is not often mentioned in the Hebrew Bible, and the majority of references are allusions to this plague.

The theme of a distinction recurs, but now it is carried further. Now it is not just the Israelites in Goshen who are spared the effects of the plague; those of Pharaoh's own subjects who *feared the warning of the* LORD could escape the effects of the plague by taking shelter themselves and bringing *the herds under cover*. (We have already noted that this dramatic account is not concerned by the claim that 'all the livestock of Egypt' had died in v. 6.) This theme, of a differentiation among Pharaoh's own subjects, will continue to be significant right down to the Exodus itself. Whereas in v. 19 the command was apparently addressed to individuals not to remain in the open, by v. 20 social distinctions have manifested themselves, and the concern is with *slaves* not brought into shelter. They were regarded as property, just as were the cattle.

9. 22–26   After the extended introduction we are now told of the plague itself, with *thunder* and *fire flashing* (presumably lightning) as well as the hail. As far as the Egyptians are concerned it is universal in its impact. The unique severity of this storm, first mentioned in v. 18, is stressed again at v. 24, but the differentiation among the Egyptians promised in vv. 19–20 is not found in the fulfilment. Instead, *everything in the fields, both man and beast* is *struck down*, whereas *Goshen* is unaffected.

9. 27–35   Pharaoh's admission is couched in legal rather than religious terms; though REB, like most modern translations, has *I have*

sinned, the language is really that of the law-court, an admission of guilt. Another new theme is then introduced: the Israelites are to go, and to waste no time about it. But *Moses* will not be hurried; he must first leave *the city*, which might be another way of referring to Pharaoh's palace but probably envisages a larger area. Only then will he *spread out* his *hands in prayer*, an expression used to denote the solemnity of what is being undertaken. The ominous remark that Pharaoh and his *subjects . . . do not yet fear the* LORD *God* clearly implies that there are more plagues to come. The 'LORD God' is an unusual expression, very rare outside the creation accounts of Gen. 2–3, but it scarcely seems likely that an allusion to that story is intended here.

Vv. 31–32 are bracketed by REB. It seems as if they reflect an early awareness of the problem we have noted; if the earlier plagues had been so devastating, what was left to be destroyed by the locusts which are shortly to appear? The *barley* is said to be *in the ear*, Hebrew *'abib*, the name which was given in the earlier Hebrew calendar to the March–April period later known as 'Nisan'. This explanatory note not only makes the story more plausible, but it also provides a link with the specification of Abib as the month of the Exodus (13. 4). On the other hand, it does lessen the dramatic effect of the story, for the hail-storm now seems to have lost its unique character.

The end of the account is predictable enough. Moses prayed as he had promised, whereupon the storms ceased (*rain* had not been specified in the earlier description but was no doubt implied), and *Pharaoh remained obdurate*. We are now told that some at least of Pharaoh's *courtiers* shared *his obduracy* – perhaps a forewarning of their punishment in the actual Exodus.

10. 1–2   Before the next plague, an unusual feature is introduced. The purpose of *Pharaoh* being *obdurate* is not only that there may be *signs* which demonstrate God's power. It is also *so that you can tell your children and grandchildren the story*. An older generation of scholars commonly envisaged this recitation as taking place around the campfire, but that rather romantic picture has now generally been abandoned, with the recognition that Israel was never in historical times a nomadic people. It is more likely that the reference is to liturgical celebrations, in which the Lord's victory over Egypt will have been a major theme, as is shown by frequent references to the Exodus in the Psalms. Liturgy is not always edifying, and it will have been important for the Israelites to be reassured that their

God had *toyed with the Egyptians* – had humiliated, or made fools of them.

10. 3–6   This time *Moses and Aaron* (introduced somewhat unexpectedly here; the remainder of this episode appears to have only Moses in mind) go *to Pharaoh* without previous divine instructions. Once again *tomorrow* is the key time, and perhaps we should see in this theme a link with the hope frequently expressed in the Psalms that deliverance would come in the morning (e.g. Ps. 30. 5). On this occasion the threat is of *locusts*, which undoubtedly in the ancient world and well into modern times have constituted a major threat to crops in Egypt. Vv. 5–6 spell out in vivid detail the extent of the plague and the damage it would cause. A slightly unusual feature is the reference to the previous plague; even *the remnant left by the hail* will be consumed. This time there is no dialogue; Moses simply 'turned his back' *and left Pharaoh's presence*.

10. 7–11   The focus at first is not on the division between Pharaoh and Moses, but on the tension within the royal court. Real Egyptian courtiers would scarcely have spoken to their master, with his claims to divinity, in the terms set out here! Their words were enough to have *Moses and Aaron . . . brought back*, and a new theme is now introduced. If the Israelites were given permission to worship, who was to be involved? REB may give a slightly misleading impression here; the point seems to be not that Pharaoh actually granted permission, but he was seeking clarification. Certainly he did not envisage the departure of the whole community, whereas that was exactly what Moses did envisage: *Everyone* was to *keep the Lord's pilgrim-feast*. This term was normally used to refer to the three great festivals of the Israelite year, and so it seems likely that we have here an anticipation of Passover, with its particular concern for the involvement of the whole family.

V. 10 is difficult. NEB saw in it Pharaoh changing his mind, first saying that all the people might go, and then limiting permission in v. 11 to the *menfolk* only. REB has changed that, stressing Pharaoh's continuing suspicion of their motives. Another possibility is that he is pictured as speaking ironically; the Hebrew is too cryptic for certainty to be possible. Most translations are agreed that the end of this verse refers to *some sinister purpose*, and this may well be right, though the idiom is not found elsewhere. The Hebrew is literally 'evil is before you' as in AV. The episode ends inconclusively, with permission apparently given but not taken up, for the menfolk to go to worship.

10. 12–15   The plague of *locusts* already threatened in v. 4 now comes about. There are links with the plague of *hail*; the locusts destroy whatever had been left by the hail, and this plague, like the earlier one, is described as so severe that *the like had never been seen before, nor ever will be again*. The actual structure of the two accounts is also very similar; thus vv. 12–13 here are very close to 9. 22–23. Whether the movement of locusts was in fact related to particular winds is disputed; they were searching for food. But the picturing of God raising *a wind roaring in from the east* certainly adds to the drama of the account.

10. 16–20   The consequences of the plague of locusts, like the account of the plague itself, are very similar to those in the description of the hail. Once again it is unlikely that Pharaoh's *I have sinned* should be seen in primarily religious terms; the language is legal. The reversal of the plague is described in remarkably summary fashion. On Moses' intercession, the wind becomes a *westerly gale* (literally a 'sea wind', reflecting a Palestinian viewpoint), and all *the locusts* were *swept into the Red Sea*. This is 'Yam Suph', literally the 'Sea of Reeds', the identity and function of which will concern us in chs 14–15. It looks as if a deliberate linkage with the Exodus event is being set up here, as we approach the end of the plague stories. Another interesting wordplay in this section, impossible to convey in English, lies in the fact that the same verb is used for *forgive* at v. 17, and *carried away* at v. 19. The usage is so unusual that it must surely have been deliberate. The section ends with Pharaoh's obstinacy directly attributed to *the LORD*. Here, as often, the concern of the Hebrew Bible to attribute all responsibility to God has consequences which modern readers may well, indeed surely should, find unacceptable.

10. 21–23   Pharaoh's obstinacy leads to another plague, described without any preliminaries. To have Egypt engulfed in *pitch darkness* is an affliction of a different kind from those that have preceded. Many of them were more life-threatening; this induces terror. It may have been envisaged as a struggle against Egyptian gods such as Amun-Re, the sun god. It is not clear why this plague should have lasted *for three days*, as against the normal pattern in which the end of the plague was dependent upon negotiation between Pharaoh and Moses and Aaron.

Christian readings from a later period took the three-day rule of darkness as an important clue in interpreting the period between the death and resurrection of Jesus. The episode ends with yet another note concerning the distinction between the experience of the Egyptians and *the Israelites*.

10. 24–29   The author does not intend us to ask how *Pharaoh* could summon *Moses* if he and his courtiers were in impenetrable darkness. Rather, we are invited to look back to vv. 10–11. Now *dependants* will be allowed to leave, but *flocks and herds must remain*. The dominant theme here is clearly Egypt's need of Israelite labour, which would be guaranteed if they had to return for their possessions. The other motif found elsewhere in the story, the desire to be rid of the Israelites, has disappeared here.

Characteristically, as success approaches the demands made by Moses are increased. A new motif is introduced: that the Egyptians must *supply . . . animals for sacrifice and whole-offering*. There is no suggestion here that the sacrifice might be contaminated by the alien origin of the victims. Instead, we have a variant on the theme of 'spoiling the Egyptians' developed at the beginning of ch. 11. If we are to take the latter part of v. 26 (*we cannot tell how we are to worship the* LORD) literally, it is scarcely compatible with a request to carry out traditional observances; but this is probably a deliberate literary device to emphasize the humiliation of the Egyptians.

The conclusion of the section begins in the familiar way, with *Pharaoh obstinate*, but then develops in a new direction. Previously Moses has apparently been able to have ready access to Pharaoh. Now there is to be a great divide between them. The dramatic irony here is inescapable. Pharaoh warns Moses that *you do not see my face again, for on the day you do, you die* (REB's wording is not well-chosen; try reading the last few words aloud!). The truth is of course the reverse: the death will be that of all the firstborn of Egypt (12. 31). Only a very literalist reading will be disturbed by the fact that Moses apparently encounters Pharaoh again in 11. 4–7.

11. 1–3   Chapter 11 functions as a transition from the account of the plagues to that of the Passover and deliverance, the Exodus itself, which will occupy us up to ch. 15. It looks as if a link with what has preceded arises immediately with the reference to *one last plague*, and this may indeed be true. But it is noteworthy that the word used here to describe the plague is not found elsewhere in Exodus, though it

does occur at Gen. 12. 17, where 'the LORD inflicted plagues on Pharaoh and his household on account of Abram's wife Sarai'. It may well be that a deliberate linkage with that other tradition is here intended.

The image in the latter part of v. 1 has been interpreted in various ways. REB likens the departure to *a man dismiss*ing *a rejected bride*, which would be an interesting reflection of an androcentric society, but this simile is not found elsewhere in the Hebrew Bible and most versions have interpreted the Hebrew quite differently. Thus NRSV simply has 'he will drive you away'. The REB interpretation is ingenious, but perhaps too much so.

The theme of the next verses is, however, clear enough. The 'spoiling of the Egyptians', forecast in 3. 21–22, now takes place, and the moral difficulties implicit in the earlier passage are very much present. There is no suggestion that the *jewellery* is simply going to be borrowed; and indeed the ethical difficulty is increased by the assertion that it is *the Lord* himself who *made the Egyptians well disposed*. The last part of v. 3 seems to be a kind of parenthesis, stressing the esteem in which *Moses* was held. As we have seen, the development of the story prevents Moses from being pictured as a hero, since God himself is in control of events, but Moses' stature must not be lessened.

11. 4–8 *Moses* is here pictured in prophetic terms, giving an oracle from God. But to whom? It is not clear whom he is addressing. It would be natural for us to assume that it is the community of Israel, who have not been referred to directly since ch. 5, but the end of the section makes it clear that he has been speaking to Pharaoh, despite the assertion of 10. 29.

In any case the message clearly presages the events which will reach a climax with the Exodus itself. A key verb in the next few chapters is the Hebrew *yaṣa'*, meaning to go out. It can have an adversative sense: God will *go out* against those who oppose him, as here in v. 4; it is also frequently found in its causative form ('bring out') of God's action on behalf of Israel.

The last and most devastating plague is here announced. The threat underlying 4. 22–23 is now to be carried out, in even more terrible form. Not just *the firstborn of Pharaoh*, as threatened in the earlier passage, but *all the firstborn of Egypt* are to *die*. The lowest in the social ranking (*the slave-girl at the handmill*) will not escape; even *the firstborn of the cattle* are to suffer. In the plague stories leading up to this point (e.g. 9. 20), a differentiation has been made between 'good' Egyptians and those who were obstinate; and the cattle were of course simply pictured as indiscriminate victims. Now the thirst for vengeance removes all niceties; all Egypt is to suffer alike.

It is not surprising that such appalling events should evoke *a great cry*, but it is not in order to engage our sympathy that this detail is included. The claim to uniqueness found here has already been a feature of the description of hail and locusts (9. 24; 10. 6). It may have been a cultic feature, wishing to stress that the events that the liturgy was commemorating were without parallel. In any case the theme of distinction between Egypt and Israel is brought out again (cf. 8. 22; 9. 4), this time in a rather curious way: while Egypt is crying *throughout all Israel no sound will be heard*. No room for sympathy here – an ironic contrast with the Egyptians being 'well disposed' to the Israelites in v. 3. The reference to the silence of the *dogs* reminds us that in the world of the Hebrew Bible dogs were not pets but scavengers which would certainly have been expected to howl at the events that were going on. In fact this may not be the sense; the Hebrew refers not to barking but to their 'moving the tongue' (cf. AV), which may be a proverbial saying or possibly a curse formula. (Only in the apocryphal book of Tobit [6. 1] is the dog pictured as its master's faithful companion, accompanying him on his journey.)

V. 8 clearly has Moses in the presence of Pharaoh, and the verb *yaṣaʾ* (cf. v. 4 above) is used three times in this one verse: REB, naturally enough, offers different English words, but we should bear in mind that *go away, go,* and *left* are all forms of the same Hebrew verb. Just as Moses leaves Pharaoh, so will Israel leave Egypt.

11. 9–10   This brief section serves as a transition. It refers back to 7. 3, reminding us that it had there been announced that *Pharaoh* would be *obstinate* despite all the *portents*. We are now to expect *still more portents*.

Institution of the Passover
12. 1–12. 36

12. 1–10   The sequel is in fact completely unexpected. Instead of a dramatic development of more portents along the lines just promised, we turn to an elaborate spelling out of liturgical requirements for a religious community. Some scholars have suggested that the basic structure of Exodus 1–15 should be seen as the story to accompany a

religious ceremony, the details of which are now spelt out. It is an interesting theory, but lacks specific supporting evidence. For our purposes, we can note the dramatic effect of such a retardation, and we are reminded that the detailed religious requirements laid down in, for example, chs 25–31 are not so distant from the actual story of the Exodus as we might suppose.

It is often held that in ancient Israel a change took place with regard to the beginning of the year. Before the Babylonian period (seventh–sixth centuries BCE), it is thought, the year was held to begin in the autumn; from then on a spring new year became the norm. If that is so (and scholars are sharply divided on the issue) then v. 2 could be seen as support for the change: what follows are the requirements for observing Passover, and that festival occurs in Nisan (March–April), which would be *the first month of the year*. (We should notice that in some respects Jews still observe autumn as the time of 'new year'; their formal dating of years from creation assumes an autumn new year, as does the ceremony of Rosh Hashanah, 'the beginning of the year'.)

That Israel is here being pictured as a religious group is underlined by the description of them as an *ʿedah*, REB *community*, but NRSV more satisfactorily 'congregation'. No explanation is offered why the ceremony should begin *on the tenth day*, nor of why the animal, once chosen, should be kept *until the fourteenth day*. Our story-world has changed; there was no reference to particular months in the accounts of the plagues. Nor have we previously been told about the Israelite *family* or *household*. But it is within such a context that Passover has continued to be observed, despite later attempts within the period covered by the Hebrew Bible to make it into a national occasion (II Kings 23. 21–23). We remember that when Jesus went to observe Passover in Jerusalem he did so, not as part of a vast national assembly but in a particular room set apart for him and his 'household' of followers (Mark 14. 12–16). The details of this are worked out in v. 4, with the stress being, not on whether there would be enough *lamb* to go round, but that there would be enough people to consume it wholly.

V. 5 is the first biblical passage to lay down the requirements concerning the victims that were to be offered. Great stress is laid on the need for such victims to be *without blemish*. In a subsistence economy, such as ancient Israel was, one might have supposed that people would often feel that a blemished animal might be offered in sacrifice to God, yet only once in the Hebrew Bible (Mal. 1. 8) is that criticism offered. There are many attacks in the prophets on the practice of sacrifice, yet with that one exception they never accuse the people of bringing blemished victims. The *sheep* and the *goats* were pastured together, as they still were in NT times (Matt. 25. 32).

The reference to *the fourteenth day*, first found here, has had great repercussions in later religious history, for it has shaped the dating both of Passover in the Jewish tradition and of Easter in the Christian church. In the early Christian church there was a group known as 'Quartodecimans', who insisted on observing Easter on the fourteenth day of Nisan, whatever day of the week it occurred. The original reason for this day being deemed so important is quite unknown to us. Controversy has also raged about the meaning of the phrase 'between the evenings', translated here *between dusk and dark*. The animals are to be killed by an approved manner of ritual *slaughter*, and here once again we are introduced to a theme which has continued to be of great importance in different religious traditions down to the present day.

Thus far in this section the situation of the Israelites in Egypt seems totally irrelevant, but at v. 7, before the description of the meal itself, an important ritual requirement is laid down which will be of vital significance when the story is resumed. *Blood* from the victims is to be *smeared on the doorposts and the lintel* of the houses where the Israelites are gathered. It looks very much as if this particular detail of the story is developed so as to supply an explanation of this otherwise very obscure rite.

We then return to the requirements of the festival. Not all the details laid down here were in fact followed in later Jewish practice, and so a distinction came to be drawn between this 'Egyptian passover' and the commands of Sinai, which later came to be normative. *Unleavened bread and bitter herbs* are now mentioned for the first time, without explanation, though unleavened bread will be very important at vv. 14–17. In v. 9 there is a strict prohibition against eating the meat *boiled*, even though in Deut. 16. 7 that is the way the lamb is to be prepared. (REB avoids this contradiction by translating the verb here as 'boil' but in Deuteronomy as 'cook'.) It seems likely that different groups which came together as Israel had different practices with regard to their festivals, and what we have in our Bible is the attempt, not wholly successful, to draw them together into one coherent set of requirements.

For the moment those requirements end with great stress on the completeness of the rite: everything is to be consumed. V. 10 reads oddly, for it appears to envisage that the strict prohibition, *You are not to leave any of it till morning*, will not be obeyed, for provision is immediately made for the disposal of what is *left over*. The illogicality can be explained either by saying that human nature doesn't change, and prohibitions get ignored, or by appeal to the relatively rare use of conditional forms in Hebrew.

12. 11–13. The preceding verses have been almost entirely concerned with cultic requirements; now we return to the situation of the community in Egypt. This is not to be a religious festival observed at leisure, but the people are to be ready for immediate movement. All is to be done in *urgent haste*. The fact that *it is the Lord's Passover* seems to be given as a reason for this haste.

The significance of the name of the festival, *pesaḥ*, is much disputed. It is clearly linked with the verb, *pasaḥ*, found in v. 13 and translated *pass over*. Scholars differ sharply as to whether the etymology of the word is significant. Two meanings have been proposed for the verb: 'to limp', as in I Kings 18. 21 where the people are accused of 'limping between two opinions' (REB: 'sit on the fence'); and 'to spare', as in Isa. 31. 5. It is possible to elicit some explanation from either of these meanings. It could involve some 'limping' rite, as the destroyer jumps over the houses marked with the sign of the blood. Or the sense of 'spare' would make good sense. But each of these explanations seems very forced, and it may well be that the spring festival had been known from time immemorial as Passover, and our present story is one explanation of the origin of that name.

The festival is clearly linked with the threat set out at 11. 4–6 and here reiterated. Now more specifically than elsewhere in the story the struggle is asserted to be between Yahweh and *all the gods of Egypt*. For once there is no reference to Pharaoh. It is not clear what to *execute judgment* upon gods would imply; either their incompetence is shown, as is frequently claimed in Isa. 40–48, or they are in some way to be involved in the punishment meted out upon their worshippers.

In any case this section is linked with the preceding one by the reference to *the blood*, and the purpose of the rite laid down in v. 7. The Israelites will be spared the *mortal blow*. It seems here that Yahweh himself is the destroyer, and this mode of reference continues to be found alongside other passages which speak of 'the destroyer', e.g. at v. 23.

12. 14–17   Before these dramatic developments, however, we return once more to the setting out of cultic requirements for community observance. It is not at all clear what is meant by *this day*, particularly because all the subsequent events take place at night. Perhaps 'day' is not to be limited to a period of twenty-four hours, but is a more general way of referring to the whole *pilgrim-feast*. It is to be a *day of remembrance*. The idea of remembering is very important in both Jewish and Christian liturgy. Just as Christian eucharistic liturgy is claimed as a remembrance of the Last Supper of Jesus with his disciples, so here it is very strongly stressed that what is being described is not simply a 'one-off' occasion, but is to be a *statute for all time*. Not just the community delivered from Egypt, but all their successors, are to observe Passover.

Or was it 'Passover'? The remainder of this section abandons that terminology and stresses instead the importance of *unleavened bread*. In post-biblical Jewish custom Passover and Unleavened Bread have been integrated into one festival, and to some extent this is already happening in the different biblical accounts of the festivals to be observed. But it is not difficult to see that two rather different themes are being brought together. Passover, with the requirement that an appropriate lamb be offered, is essentially the festival of a shepherding community; the command to eat Unleavened Bread ties in much more with the life-cycle of an agricultural group whose year was shaped by the availability of the crops. Here in Exodus 12, though we are mainly concerned with the final form of the narrative, it is not difficult to see distinct emphases, and our present section is very much an 'Unleavened Bread' section, whereas in vv. 1–10 'unleavened bread' had warranted no more than a passing mention (v. 8).

In the present context the community is given timeless instructions concerning the importance of *ridding your houses of leaven* – an instruction which seems quite irrelevant to their situation in Egypt. Instead they are being addressed as a *sacred assembly*, the rules for which are carefully spelt out. In v. 15 the order of phrases is not clear; REB, like other English versions, implies that law-breakers will be permanently excluded from the community, but it would be possible to read the clauses in a different order so that we have 'is to be expelled from Israel from the first day until the seventh', that is, not allowed to participate in the festival. The rules concerning work that may be done seem to be less strict than those which would later apply to Sabbath; here it *will be allowed . . . to provide food*.

The section ends by bringing us back to the situation in Egypt, though the departure is here pictured in terms quite different from anything we have encountered so far. Now Yahweh is pictured as delivering the people *in your tribal hosts* – a military metaphor far removed from either the picture of departure for a religious ceremony or of an escape during a time of confusion.

12. 18–20 The requirements for the festival are spelt out here as if they were future, but in fact entirely from a later viewpoint. Its dates are laid down, and equally important, the participants are identified. Observance is to extend to both *foreigner and native*, though we shall notice at v. 45 that more precise restrictions are laid down on non-native participation. The viewpoint here is entirely Palestinian; the 'foreigners' were those who were living among the Israelites when they were established in their land. But for the Israelites themselves they were bound to observe these requirements *wherever you live*.

12. 21–27 After all these liturgical specifications we return to the dramatic narrative, and we note that it is here *Moses* alone who receives the instructions. Aaron had been present for the more specific religious requirements. The command to *slaughter the Passover* reads oddly; presumably this refers to *the lambs*. Either this implies a pre-existing knowledge of what 'the Passover' implied, or we are intended to apply what we were told in vv. 1–10. But previous requirements concerning the killing and eating of the victim are now supplemented by instructions of a very different kind. The herb that was to be taken has traditionally been understood as 'hyssop', an English term derived from the Hebrew word used here. But REB *marjoram* is more likely to be right. The instructions outlined briefly in v. 7 are now spelt out more fully, culminating in the requirement not to *go outside the door of your house*.

The reason for that restriction is immediately given. Yahweh is about to *go throughout Egypt and strike it*, making exception only for those houses where *he sees the blood*. In that case he will *pass over*; once again we have the verb *pasaḥ*, as in v. 13 above. A double wordplay seems to be intended here. Not only are we reminded of the feast of *pesaḥ*, but also the word *door* is *pethaḥ*. It appears here as if Yahweh is guiding operations; the actual destructive work is to be done by an agent simply referred to as *the destroyer*.

In this context the last part of our section is unexpected. What seem to be emergency measures for a crisis now become a *perpetual ordinance*. It is a long time since the people's departure from Egypt has

51

been linked to the *promised . . . land*, but that is now the context. The theme of *children asking* the meaning of the rites being observed is found in Deut. 6. 20, and, if we were to explore origins it is quite likely that our present passage has been elaborated by a Deuteron-omistic editor. Certainly the custom of children asking the meaning of the Passover rite has survived in Jewish practice. It is striking that the word *'abodah*, previously used to refer to the labour required of the people by the Egyptians (5. 11), is now used of a religious service: REB *observance*.

In v. 27 the feast is described most unusually as a 'Passover sacrifice', though REB obscures this by not translating the word 'sacrifice'. Once again we have the verb *pasaḥ* used of divine activity. Here it clearly has the implication of 'spared'. The whole episode is set firmly in a cultic context by the concluding sentence: *the people bowed low in worship*.

12. 28–30   This section begins by noting the people's obedient response. We should bear it in mind, for much of the subsequent nar-rative, both in Exodus and in Numbers, will be concerned with the people's *dis*obedience. In the immediate context, of course, the sharp distinction between Israelites and Egyptians is being stressed, for the devastating fate of *all the firstborn in Egypt* is now announced. Modern readers with any sensitivity will be thankful for the brief summary nature of the statement, without any detailed embellishment, unlike the rather comic description of, for example, the plague of frogs (8. 1–4). The structure of the Hebrew sentence stresses particularly that it was *the Lord* who *struck down* all the victims. We are left to reflect for ourselves on the appalling ways in which human imagination can envisage divine action. At the literary level this brief statement matches the threat in 11. 4–6, with one detail changed: the lowest level of society is now represented not by the slave-girl but by *the prisoner in the dungeon*.

12. 31–36   This time there is no mistaking that *Pharaoh* means what he says; they are to *be off*. The death of the firstborn is clearly pictured here as the climax of the previous plagues. Pharaoh's permission to depart is not given simply because of the devastating effect of the plague, but in terms of *worship . . . as you request*, though *the Egyptians* at large, in v. 33, seem to have more sense of the desperate situation. As against the limited permission of 10. 24 *flocks and herds* may now be taken, and the earlier requests for prayer are now put more strongly:

ask God's blessing on me. We are reminded of Gen. 12. 3, where 'all the peoples on earth' are to be blessed through Abraham's descendants. The use of the verb *urged* is also noteworthy; for it is a form of the same word used to describe Pharaoh's hardness of heart.

V. 34 provides a narrative context for what had previously been unexplained commands. Eating the Passover in haste, and taking *dough before it was leavened* are now set in the context of urgent departure. The rare word *kneading troughs* reminds us of the way the Egyptian troughs had been invaded by frogs (8. 3); no such problem now! The section ends with the gleeful spelling out of the 'spoiling of the Egyptians', as forecast in 11. 2–3. It is a thoroughly unattractive episode; the Egyptians are pictured as *well disposed*, which seems simply to mean that they were gullible. The looters took whatever they wanted, and *the Egyptians were plundered.* This may be regarded as one of the negative aspects of a liberation reading of this story; once liberated the victims behave just as vindictively as their former oppressors. If God could kill Egyptians, his people could rob them.

The Exodus from Egypt

12. 37–15. 21

The Israelites' departure
12. 37–13. 22

12. 37–39 As the REB sub-heading indicates we are now at the beginning of the account of the Exodus itself. It begins *from Rameses*, already familiar to readers as a symbol of oppression from the reference in 1. 11. The first stage of the journey was to *Succoth*, which is not likely to be an Egyptian name as it is the ordinary Hebrew word for 'booths'. Some place in Egypt might have been known by Israelites under this name, or there may be a deliberate allusion to Palestinian places of the same name. The departure of the Israelites is pictured very much as that of an army. The verb translated *set out* has the sense of 'broke camp', and the numbers of a vast army are then indicated. So far the Israelites have been pictured as a small group of day-labourers, centred in one restricted area, and living in dread of their Egyptian overlords. Nothing in the narrative so far has prepared us for a body of *six hundred thousand men on foot*. In the mid-Victorian age Bishop Colenso wrote a detailed study, which caused great offence by spelling out in rather prosaic detail some of the logistical problems which would be caused by such a force attempting to traverse the desert, referring to such matters as climate, food supply and the necessary sanitary arrangements. We need not go into such detail for it to be clear that the numbers cannot be taken literally. Various attempts have been made to suppose that 'six hundred thousand' actually means 'six hundred military units', but all such attempts break down at some point. For the purposes of the story the narrator wanted us to envisage this huge host, and we must recognize that it cannot be taken out of that story-world into a real historical world.

The six hundred thousand men are not alone. They are accompanied by *women and children*, and also by a *large company of others*, the 'mixed multitude' of traditional translations. We are given no indication as to who these people may have been, though speculation has run riot. Their presence accounts for the fact that in the remainder of the Pentateuch reference is sometimes made to those who were not full members of the community (e.g. Num. 11. 4). The section ends with a somewhat different picture of the people's departure from Egypt. Here they have *been driven out*, told, as it were, to go away, even before they could *get food ready for themselves*. This is not the kind of thing that can be done with an army of six hundred thousand men!

12. 40–42   One strand in the material seems to be aware that history needs dates. There are many such in Genesis, but rather few so far in Exodus. Now we are told that the Israelites' stay in Egypt, presumably from the time of Joseph, had been *four hundred and thirty years to the very day*. It is not clear what is envisaged by the 'very day ' of their arrival, and – whatever the origin of the four hundred and thirty-year tradition – no modern historian has found it a reliable basis for reconstruction. The same self-understanding as wishes to spell out the history also wants to stress the totality of Israelite presence in Egypt; not a small body of nomads, but *all the tribes of the Lord*. But this was in any case not what we should call secular history; it was a way for the later community to claim that all its forebears had gone through what we might call the 'Exodus experience'. In the story it was to be observed by means of a cultic *vigil*.

12. 43–47   We are not surprised, therefore, that this and the immediately following sections depart from these 'historical' concerns in order to spell out the religious requirements imposed upon the community. Who may participate in the Passover? Not the *foreigner*, a prohibition which reminds us of the disputes of the Second Temple period reflected in parts of Isaiah and in Ezra-Nehemiah. But the *bought slave* (male, of course) might take part provided he had been *circumcised*. Here clearly we are a long way from an oppressed community in Egypt. Those being addressed were in a position in a social hierarchy which enabled them to oppress others by buying them as slave-labour. The *visitor* would not be in such a degrading situation; perhaps those engaged in trade are envisaged. Finally we have *the hired man*, the equivalent of the contemporary *Gastarbeiter* in Germany and elsewhere, who is excluded from participation. Stress is then laid on the domestic character of Passover, which is particularly emphasized in Exodus, whereas Deut. 16 is more concerned to centralize the observance. We have already noted the ambivalent

nature of the celebration in New Testament times (see the commentary on vv. 1–10 above). A previously unmentioned prohibition is that on *breaking any of* the *bones* of the Passover lamb. Concern for this commandment was still found in the Dead Sea Scrolls, and was regarded as so important by the author of the Fourth Gospel that it was quoted as the climax to the Passion story (John 19. 36). Having laid down these rules as to its boundaries, then *the whole community of Israel* is to engage in Passover. Needless to say, all the groups which have been mentioned are male.

12. 48–49   These two verses seem to be a kind of appendix to what has preceded. They are set out in the form of case-law (*If . . . then*), of a type with which we shall become familiar in chs 21–23. It seems as if a case had arisen: might an *alien* participate in Passover if not all of the male members of his family had been circumcised? No: all the group (its extent is not defined) must have been circumcised before any could participate.

12. 50–51   The chapter is rounded off in a very satisfactory way from an Israelite point of view. V. 28 is repeated to stress the people's obedience, and *the day* is that spelt out in v. 41.

13. 1–2   We have already seen in the latter part of ch. 12 that the drama of mass slaughter and hasty departure has given way to the sonorous and timeless spelling out of liturgical requirements, and vv. 1–16 of this chapter detain us in that same religious world. These first two verses stand somewhat apart, being concerned with the *firstborn*, literally 'that which opens the womb'. The basic principle of *dedication* is set out here; what that implied is spelt out both later in this chapter (vv. 11–13) and at 22. 29–30 and 34. 19–20. The passage must be seen in the context of Israel being described as God's firstborn (4. 22), and the destruction of all Egypt's firstborn.

13. 3–10   The observances of the Festival of Unleavened Bread associated with the deliverance from Egypt are not to be a 'one-off' event; they are to be maintained when the Lord has brought the people to *the land which he swore to your forefathers to give you*. The month of the celebration is named here as *Abib*, probably the older name which was later replaced as a month-name by 'Nisan'. The picture is of a universal observance, so much so that in v. 7 we find the very idealistic but rather impractical command that *nothing fermented or leavened*

must be seen throughout your territory. The family basis is maintained with the requirement that the *son* of each family is to have explained to him the reason for the festival. The – surely figurative – language of v. 9 has been taken literally by observant Jews into modern times. They still mark *hand* and *forehead* in the way they take to be required here.

13. 11–13   The implications of dedicating the *firstborn* to Yahweh are now spelt out. Whereas in v. 2 it might have seemed that all firstborn, human and animal, were to be treated similarly, now important distinctions are made. In particular the *donkey*, valuable as a beast of burden, is to be *redeemed*. It is important to recognize that this word does not have special theological overtones in this context; it means 'bought back', that is, from God, to whom it belongs, and the price is a *kid or lamb*. The alternative possibility of *breaking its neck* is allowed for, but one cannot suppose that this was often done. Finally, of course, all human firstborn were to be bought back. It is most unlikely that human sacrifice was regularly resorted to among the communities known to Israel, but if it was, then no such practice was acceptable to the worshippers of Yahweh.

13. 14–16   This whole section (13. 1–16) has often been thought to have links with Deuteronomy. The preaching style of Deuteronomy often embodies repetition, and this is well illustrated here. The instruction of the *son*, the meaning of what has happened, the record on *hand* and *forehead* are all repeated from earlier in the chapter. The only new emphasis is the specific link between the punishment of the Egyptians and the redeeming of Israel's firstborn sons.

13. 17–18   The double spacing in REB follows the divisions in the Hebrew Bible itself and alerts us to the fact that we now revert to the basic story. Rather unexpectedly the departure is pictured as *Pharaoh* letting *the people go*; we seem to be back with a small group, easily intimidated *when war confronts them*, not the vast army of six hundred thousand men. In any case an important new theme is introduced. So far we know that the Israelites have been led out of Egypt, at least 'on the way to Succoth' (12. 37). Where next? The natural way to the land they had been promised would be along the much-travelled route near the Mediterranean coast, literally 'the way of the land of the Philistines' (REB: *the road leading toward the Philistines*). This way of describing the route would be anachronistic if we were trying to give

a plausible historical setting for the Exodus, but if, as seems more likely, we should read the book as the product of a later age, then this would have been the natural description.

In any case it is not the route to be taken. Whereas elsewhere the long detour *by way of the wilderness* is pictured as punishment, here it is a means of saving the people from the risk that they might *change their minds* if troubles arose. This anxiety about a possible desire to return to Egypt occurs a number of times in the Hebrew Bible (in the very next chapter, 14. 11–12, and also in Num. 11 and 14), and is associated with dissatisfaction with life in the wilderness. There is a sense in which the events from now on are better seen as part of the wilderness tradition than as integral to the deliverance from Egypt. Once again (cf. 10. 19) we get a reference to the *Red Sea*. At least for the final narrator it is clear that this stretch of water was not near the Mediterranean coast, but no positive clues are yet offered. The meaning of the last phrase of v. 18 is uncertain. REB, like NEB, follows the Greek translation with a reference to *the fifth generation*, but we have had no previous hints of such a classification. It may be better to see a meaning 'prepared for battle' as in NRSV.

13. 19   This verse offers one of the few links back to the story of the ancestors. Here we have an allusion to, rather than a direct quotation of, Gen. 50. 24–25.

13. 20–22   Now the community has left Egypt and has reached *the edge of the wilderness*. The whereabouts of *Etham* are unknown. More important, the community are pictured as a worshipping group, assured of the divine presence. Wandering herdsmen would not normally travel at night, but the Israelites are enabled to do so, by God's guidance with a *pillar of cloud* or *of fire* as appropriate. This is the language of the theophany, as for example in Isaiah 6; it assures us that it is no ordinary journey on which the community is embarking.

The crossing of the Sea of Reeds
14. 1–15. 21

14. 1–4   The people have left Egypt, but their dealings with Pharaoh and his people are not yet over. The instruction here appears directly to contradict 13. 17, for now they are to *turn back*. But this is a divine command given via Moses to show that God's dealings with Pharaoh

are not yet complete. The people are to camp *by the sea*. The place-names are of no help in trying to be more specific in geographical terms. They are not known from any Egyptian sources, and *Baal-zephon* in particular seems much more likely to be a Canaanite than an Egyptian name. The point is that the people are pictured as *hemmed in by the wilderness*. (The exact meaning of the phrase is not clear, but the general sense is obvious enough.) In what may seem to us a most unattractive way, God is pictured as kicking Pharaoh when he is down: making him *obstinate*, and thereby winning *glory for myself at the expense of Pharaoh*. This is of course a continuation of the theme that ran right through the plague stories, and thus binds the 'Egypt' and 'wilderness' elements of the whole narrative together.

14. 5–9 It is as if the death of the firstborn had never happened; the total chaos which such an event would have caused, and which was graphically pictured in 12. 28–30, plays no part in the narrative from now on. Pharaoh, his *courtiers* and his army appear unaffected by previous disasters, and the departure of the Israelites seems to be no more than an absent-minded gesture of generosity on their part. So the army is mobilized, and set off *in pursuit* of the Israelites. Once again we have the ambiguity in the portrayal of the Israelites; sometimes a small frightened group who have managed to escape from Egyptian oppression; sometimes a religious community; sometimes a large army, as here where they *marched defiantly away*.

14. 10–14 Now the picture of the little oppressed group re-emerges. When they *looked up and saw the Egyptians* they were *in terror*. We are now introduced to a theme which will recur in the stories of the wilderness. In the face of some evil, the people cry out to God, blaming their leaders and sometimes God also for the trouble that has come upon them. There is no recollection of the evils they had suffered or of the great deliverance that God had wrought on the people's behalf; instead they would have been better off *as slaves to the Egyptians*. But Moses, guided by God, promises that the problem, be it an enemy army, or lack of food and water, will be resolved. It is a theme we shall meet again in ch. 16, and it recurs frequently in the book of Numbers. We need not suppose that the apparent 'quote' in v. 12 actually refers to anything earlier in the book; this is a literary device effectively employed to heighten the dramatic effect. The episode ends by introducing another theme which modern readers may, indeed should, find difficult: that of 'holy war'. In the ancient

world it was customary to picture gods as being like kings (cf. II Sam. 11. 1) as regularly engaged in war on behalf of their people. (The picture survives in the New Testament, e.g. Luke 14. 31.) Israel's God was no exception: he will fight for you.

14. 15–18   God appears to need *Moses* as an intermediary to explain what is going on. In any case the command is clear. The Israelites are pictured as an army, being told to *strike camp*, but the real warfare is waged by God. Moses' *staff* comes into play again, as in the plague stories, and we are given a foretaste of what is to come when the rod (?and/or Moses' *hand*) have power to *divide* (the sea) *asunder*. At the moment all that is promised is a successful escape for the Israelites, who will be able to *pass through the sea on dry ground*. But the repeated phrases in vv. 17–18 fill us with the expectation that something more than that is envisaged – a final triumph *at the expense of Pharaoh and his army, chariots and cavalry all together.*

14. 19–20   We have not previously heard anything in the account of the deliverance about *the angel of God*, and such a being has no role here other than being resident in *the pillar of cloud.* Perhaps the angel's presence was necessary to explain the apparent contradiction of 13. 22, where it was stated that 'the pillar never left its place in front'. The present crisis warrants emergency measures. V. 20 is rather confusing; the Hebrew text appears to say that the cloud produced light for the Israelites and darkness for the Egyptians, but the general sense is clear enough. The Egyptians may have been 'close behind' (v. 10), but they are for the moment kept away from the Israelites.

14. 21–25   A popular 'naturalistic' explanation of what is pictured next has been to suppose that the events took place in and around the Bitter Lakes, near the present Suez Canal. It is held that *a strong east wind* might have dried up an area usually covered with water, to an extent that nomads travelling light and on foot might find safe passage, whereas the terrain would be impassable for chariots. Such a reconstruction falls foul of the same objections as we noted for the comparable explanation of the plagues. There is, first of all, the inherent implausibility of what is proposed: lightly-clad men on foot might indeed be able to go where no chariot could penetrate, but that is most unlikely to be made more feasible by particular winds. More seriously, such an explanation runs clean counter to the text which is after all our only source of knowledge. Though there are inconsistencies within the text, which we shall notice in a moment, it is wholly consistent in attributing what took place to a decisive act of God making possible what would normally be quite impossible.

The picture which has caught the modern imagination, not least in film depictions of the event, is found at the end of v. 21 and in v. 22. The waters are *divided* so that they *formed a wall to right and left of* the Israelites. All the Egyptian army *followed in pursuit*. One wonders whether at some point in the tradition Pharaoh himself was pictured as being among those who pursued, but that is not specified here. It was *in the morning watch*, the characteristic time for divine intervention, that *the Lord looked down*, as he and his companions had done over Sodom (Gen. 18. 16), as if deciding what to do. The decision was quickly reached. God *threw them into a panic*, by what means we do not know. Perhaps we should modify the order of the narrative and suppose that the clogging *of the chariot wheels* was the cause rather than the effect of the panic, but in any case the stress is on God's warlike intervention on behalf of his people. The Egyptians, like an army defeated in war, cry *Let us flee*.

14. 26–31   But it is of course too late. Before they can take any action the Egyptians are engulfed by the returning waters. This picture is somewhat at odds with what has preceded, for if the *water . . . covered all Pharaoh's army*, it will not have mattered whether or not the chariot wheels were clogged. There may be different sources underlying our final form; at least as likely is that we should see here the characteristic variants of traditional story-telling. The verb used to describe God's action is particularly vivid: literally the Lord 'shook off' the Egyptians *into the sea*. The disaster is, as any intelligent reader will have long since seen to be inevitable, absolute and total. We are a long way from history here; no disaster of this kind is known from any independent source, and the once-popular theory that the death of a few Egyptian border-guards has been magnified into the story we now have is equally far from the story told. Nor are geographical questions very relevant. Various localities have been suggested as the origin of this tradition. Hebrew 'sea of reeds' is not known to be a specific location, and the proposals put forward have ranged from the Mediterranean foreshore down to the modern Red Sea. What we have is theological geography, showing God's ability to use natural forces to bring about his will.

Vv. 29–31 provide a kind of 'happy ending' as far as the Israelites were concerned. They had been protected by the wall of water; they had been *saved from the power of Egypt*, because they saw a far greater *power* at work on their behalf. (The same word, literally 'hand' is used to describe both Egyptian and divine power.) What other possibility could there be than for the people to be *in awe of the Lord and put their faith in him*? All is well for the moment, and the jubilation will be expressed in song. But we must not expect this state of affairs to last. This happy relation between God and people was to prove very short-lived.

15. 1–21   There follows the only extended piece of poetry in Exodus, often referred to as 'the Song of the Sea'. It has attracted much atten-tion among scholars, on three grounds in particular. First, the Hebrew text has some unusual features much discussed by those concerned with textual matters. Secondly, its date has been very variously assessed. Some have supposed it to be almost contemporary with the events it describes; others have taken it as a much later composition, looking back on traditions that had by then entered Israel's sacred history. Thirdly, the relation of this piece of poetry to the preceding prose accounts is disputed. Is this the 'original' upon which the prose has drawn? Or is this a composition based upon existing prose versions? We may note, on this last point, that a similar problem arises with Judges 4 and 5, where a prose account of the defeat of Sisera is followed by a poem, the Song of Deborah, describing the same events. We shall not be able in a brief commentary of this kind to give detailed consideration to all these issues, but they need to be kept in mind as part of the background to our discussion. It is generally agreed that victory hymns of this kind were a characteristic feature of Ancient Near Eastern religious poetry; Yahweh is here celebrated as a warrior, and in this he and his worshippers were in line with the thought of their time and place.

The poem begins with ascriptions of praise to God, pictured, as we have already seen, as *a warrior*. Holy war is a frequent theme in the Hebrew Bible. The theme of *triumph* offers a recurring motif through-out the hymn (vv. 1, 7, 21). If REB is right in translating the next expression as *horse and rider* this would be a pointer to a late date for the poem, as the practice of riding horses in warfare was not known before Assyrian times. *The sea* is often regarded as a hostile element in the Hebrew Bible, but of course it could be hostile to enemies as well as to the Israelites themselves. In v. 2 older English versions have a phrase which has almost become traditional in religious language, 'the Lord is my strength and my song', but REB, like most modern translations, has *my refuge and my defence*, which makes better sense in the context.

Vv. 4–8 describe the fate of the enemy. REB retains *Red Sea* for *yam suph*, 'sea of reeds'; we have seen already that identification of a particular site is impossible. In any case the imagery of v. 5, with its references to *the watery abyss* and *the depths*, shows that this was no ordinary accident at sea, but that the dimensions of the event were cosmic. This aspect is brought out even more vividly in v. 8, where the water *piled up* and *congealed*. We should not ask in prosaic terms for a precise meaning of these expressions; this is vivid poetic imagery, whose force depends on the relentless accumulation of metaphors. This is true also of the allusions to the Egyptians' fate in the intervening verses, 6–7, *consumed . . . like stubble* in the power of God's *right hand*.

V. 9 employs a motif common to victory hymns such as this: the boasting of the enemy (cf. Judg. 5. 30). There is no logic in the boasting – fleeing Israelites would scarcely have had much *spoil* to be *divided*. But it is in any case totally vain, for without a break (Hebrew has no equivalent to quotation marks) God is again addressed and the theme of v. 5 reiterated: the enemy *sank like lead*. This first part of the hymn ends in vv. 11–12, stressing that Yahweh's power is incomparable (*Who is like you among the gods?*), and rehearsing some of his attributes.

So far the song has concentrated entirely on events at the 'sea of reeds', but vv. 13–17 take us in an unexpected direction. One reason for disputes concerning the date of the song is the reference in these verses to events that apparently occurred much later in the people's history. Though it is possible that *your holy dwelling-place* in v. 13 refers to Sinai, it is much more natural to take it as referring to Jerusalem. If this is the right understanding, then the whole poem is setting out a picture of the extended wanderings of the people before they finally claimed Jerusalem as their holy place. Some of those whom they encountered in those wanderings are then mentioned, with the clear implication that, if they were to oppose the power of Israel's God, they might expect a fate comparable to that experienced by the Egyptians. An important aspect of victory hymns of this kind was that they acted as a kind of reminder to God that his services might be needed again.

Various of Israel's traditional enemies are mentioned. The *dwellers in Philistia*, better known as the Philistines, are mostly remembered because of the warfare described in the books of Samuel, at the time of Saul and David, but they were still regarded as a threat in Jeremiah 47. *Edom* and *Moab* were traditional rivals of Judah in the area East of the

Dead Sea; in an anticipatory way their *terror and dread* are envisaged. The verbs used in vv. 14–16 are all in effect synonyms describing the inevitability of defeat for all the people's enemies. The hymn ends with a cry of confidence that Yahweh will continue and complete the victories he has inaugurated, so that vv. 17–18 have been described as 'the national anthem of ancient Israel'.

After a brief prose recapitulation, we come in v. 20 to a new character, described as *the prophetess Miriam, Aaron's sister*. We saw when looking at ch. 2 that the unnamed young woman there does not seem to have been identified with Miriam, and indeed the tradition seems to link Miriam much more closely with Aaron than with Moses (e.g. Num. 12. 1). She is described as a 'prophetess', not in the sense of giving oracles or announcing the future, but in a different sense also associated with prophecy: that of ecstatic song (cf. I Sam. 19. 18–24). Women could certainly be associated with the composition and singing of triumph songs for victory (cf. Judg. 5. 1; Ps. 68. 25), and some have seen the brief *refrain* attributed to Miriam here as being the oldest nucleus of the Song of the Sea.

One other aspect of the story of deliverance should be borne in mind. The biblical text has often appeared to show no concern for the Egyptian victims, but in later Jewish tradition this has often been a matter of concern. Thus a rabbinic tradition tells of God refusing to let the angels sing a song of praise for the destruction of the Egyptians: 'The work of my hands has been drowned in the sea, and you want to sing songs?'

The Israelites in the Wilderness
15. 22–18. 27

Feeding with manna
15. 22–16. 36

15. 22–25a   REB is right to put in a cross-heading '*In the wilderness*' at this point, for we have reached a major transition in the book. Egypt is left behind, and will scarcely be mentioned again except for a few longing recollections of the delights of life there (!). The people are going *out into the wilderness*.

These wilderness traditions predominate up to ch. 17, and it may be important to stress that the wilderness is in no way pictured as Israel's 'natural' habitat. It was once widely supposed that Israel in some way embodied the purity of desert existence confronted with the decadence of Canaan which was in thrall to the natural round of the agricultural year, and had a religious system given over to a variety of sexual excesses. Such a picture tells us more about the imagination of some scholars than about the facts of the case. The alleged excesses of Canaanite religion are not supported by neutral evidence, and Israel was essentially an agricultural society, with the wilderness pictured as alien, and time spent there a punishment.

Our present passage shows that the happy relation between God and people described at 14. 31 was short-lived. *Three days* was enough; first there was no water at all, then when some was found it was undrinkable. This produces a chain of events which will be repeated in the wilderness tradition. The people *complained* (this is the 'murmuring' of older translations), usually *to Moses*; he seeks divine guidance and, for the moment, all is well. This brief episode has an 'aetiological' element, that is, it offers an explanation of a place-name: *Marah* means *bitter*, as we remember from Naomi's cry of bitterness at Ruth 1. 20.

15. 25b–26   The next episode is unusual. It is not stated how *the* L*ORD* *laid down a statute*, or how it was known to the people (Moses does not

feature). It seems to anticipate the detailed law-giving at Sinai which is shortly to follow, and is couched in the conditional language more typical of the book of Deuteronomy. Nowhere else do we find the implicit comparison with the *sufferings* of *the Egyptians*. The link with the Marah story is provided by the description of *the* LORD as *healer*. This was the point which the book Ecclesiasticus, in the Apocrypha, seized on, seeing this as a model example of God's healing power (Ecclus. 38. 7).

15. 27 Nothing is known of *Elim*, mentioned here and at Num. 33. 9. It is clearly pictured as an oasis, a genuine haven for a small group of travellers, though the *twelve springs* would not have been adequate for the whole nation pictured in some of the traditions (cf. again 12. 37).

16. 1 One element in the editing of the book, noted already at 12. 40–42, wishes to stress that *the whole Israelite community* underwent the wilderness experience, and is also anxious to spell out detailed chronology and exact geography. The chronology provides a link back to 12. 41 and forward to 19. 1. Whether the geography was based on local knowledge of the area described is difficult to assess. Many proposals have been made for identifying *the wilderness of Sin* (an evocative name on which preachers might elaborate!) but they have to remain no more than speculation.

16. 2–8 Once again we have the 'murmuring' motif noticed already in 15. 22–25. Lack of food is the cause of complaint, and we are offered a picture of life in Egypt, where they *sat by the fleshpots and had plenty of bread*, which is in marked contrast to the hard labour described in the earlier chapters. In this episode *Moses and Aaron* are not just the recipients of the complaint; they are accused of having caused the problem.

In the development of this story, however, the element of complaint is no more than a device for introducing a whole new theme: the provision of *bread from heaven*, what has come to be known as 'manna' (v. 31). In this section the provision of this food serves not just to satisfy hunger but also to test the community's obedience. The food will be available for six days, with a double supply *on the sixth day*. The implication is clearly that the Sabbath is to be observed and no food collected on that day, but that requirement is not yet spelt out. Instead, in their reply *Moses and Aaron* revert to the theme of complaint, promising the people that they will receive not only food but also a vision of *the glory of the* LORD. Thus they deflect the people's grievance from themselves: *it is against the* LORD *that you bring your complaints, not against us.*

16. 9–12 The promises made in the previous section are now fulfilled. As in 4. 14–16 and intermittently elsewhere *Aaron* is pictured as the spokesman, explaining divine commands to the people, while *Moses* is in direct contact with God.

16. 13–20 The fulfilment of the promise starts in a somewhat un-expected way. Mention is made of *a flock of quails*. They play no further part in this story, though in Num. 11. 31–32 they are mentioned, again in a context which refers to manna, as a means of satisfying hunger. It looks as if this is a deliberate cross-reference to the story in Numbers, possibly introduced here because the promise in vv. 8 and 11 has mentioned *flesh* as well as *bread*. Originally the two words may have been intended as different ways of referring to the same thing; the final editor of the text understood it as promising two kinds of food.

The main fulfilment of the promise, however, is found in vv. 13b–16. There has been much discussion of the *fine flakes* which appeared on the ground. Various proposals have been made that they can be identified either as the excretion of some form of insect or as a particular type of gum resin. Ingenious as these explanations are, they seem to miss the point of the story in the same way as do the natural-istic explanations of the plagues of Egypt. The essential thrust of the story is that this is a wholly unique provision of food for his people by God, sufficient to feed the whole community, and with its supply miraculously ordered so that on Fridays a double quantity appears and on Saturdays none at all. In addition, though some gathered *more, some less . . . each had just as much as he could eat*. No gum resin or insect excretion meets all these criteria!

The cry of the people, *What is that?*, is to be understood therefore not simply as a request for information, but also as an indication of their failure to recognize God's favour when it was shown to them. The Hebrew of the question is *man hu'*, and it is from this that the word 'manna' is derived. It is not a 'real' Hebrew word denoting some particular plant or the like. (Other versions, e.g. NRSV, indicate this point, but it does not emerge in REB until v. 31.) The section ends with a further detail stressing the failure of the people to grasp what was going on; despite the command not *to keep any of it till morning*, some did, and *it became full of maggots and stank*. The disobedience of the people to God's commands through Moses, and the anger that this provoked, is a recurring theme in the wilderness stories.

16. 21–26   The link with the Sabbath is now brought out. On the preceding day the harvest is twofold, and the *chiefs of the community* are reassured that *what remains over* may properly be *kept until morning*. And so it proves: *it neither stank nor became infested*! The importance of proper Sabbath observance, constantly emphasized in direct divine commands, is here brought out in story form.

16. 27–30   We can guess in advance what will happen next: some of the people are disobedient and incur God's anger for failure to keep the Sabbath. For the moment, however, though his anger is aimed at the Israelites, it is confined to an address to Moses. Things will get worse before the wilderness journey is over, but those developments are found in the book of Numbers.

16. 31   The name *manna* is now found. This verse looks like an explanatory note aimed at satisfying the curiosity of a later generation concerning this remarkable food. We are to assume that *coriander seed* describes its appearance, and the *wafer made with honey* its taste, not obviously compatible with the 'butter cakes' described in Num. 11. 8.

16. 32–36   These last verses consciously look back upon the gift of manna. A specimen is to be kept in a *jar*, and placed before the *'eduth*. What exactly is meant is not very clear; REB translates it as *Testimony*, the construction of which has not yet been described. According to the understanding of the author of the Letter to Hebrews it was kept within the most holy part of the temple along with other memorabilia from the time of wilderness wandering (Heb. 9. 4). Meanwhile, the whole community relied on manna for its food *for forty years* until their arrival at the Promised Land. In this way the point is made that the Israelites were totally different from any other wandering people, who would certainly not have confined themselves to such a diet. It is pictured very specifically as 'religious food'. Various New Testament writers seized on this as an illustration of God's gifts to his followers. Sometimes it might be taken up in a positive way (Rev. 2. 17), but more characteristically to emphasize the point that in Jesus God had sent an even more powerful gift than the manna (John 6. 49–51). Paul ingeniously combined the two approaches by identifying the food given in the wilderness with Christ (I Cor. 10. 3–4). In later ages, the

theme of manna has been of great importance within the Christian tradition, especially in the way that it has been seen by liturgists and hymn-writers as a symbol of the eucharistic bread.

The chapter ends with a brief note explaining the usage of the probably obsolete term *omer* in terms with which a later generation would be more familiar.

Trials and tribulations
17. 1–18. 27

17. 1–7 A further stage in the wilderness journey is described, with consequences which we have by now come to expect. *There was no water*, and so *a dispute arose*. The people demand water; Moses responds angrily; the people once again announce that there was no point in leaving Egypt, if they were to *die of thirst*. Moses appeals to God, and receives instructions comparable with, though differing in detail from, those received in earlier crises. A link with the Egypt story is established by the requirement that Moses take with him *the staff with which* he *struck the Nile*. In a curiously homely touch God says he will be *waiting for* Moses *by a rock in Horeb*. The mention of Horeb recalls 3. 1, and Moses' first encounter with God, but the link is not developed. Water pours out, and presumably the people's thirst was quenched, but the interest of the narrative has now switched elsewhere – to the naming of the place. Unexpectedly two names are given to one spot: *Massah and Meribah*. The explanation of these names is then given in reverse order. 'Meribah' comes from a verb meaning *disputed*, and 'Massah' is a *test*. In Ps. 95. 8 these two names are used as a paradigm of the people's stubborn behaviour in the wilderness, linked there with the threat found elsewhere in the Pentateuch that virtually none of those who had been brought out of Egypt would survive to enter the Promised Land.

17. 8–13 So far the difficulties which have confronted the people following their deliverance from Egypt have been 'natural' ones, in particular the lack of food and water. Now human enemies are encountered. *The Amalekites* may have been alluded to earlier in lists (e.g. Gen. 36. 12, 16), but this is their first appearance in a narrative. They continue to be pictured as the people's enemies, in the wilderness (e.g. Num. 14), in the time of settlement (Judg. 6–7) and when the monarchy was established (I Sam. 15). Neither this story nor any of

the other references to them are of much help in giving a historical or geographical setting for the Amalekites; they are pictured as typifying the enemies of the people, and against them the most appalling vengeance was to be taken (cf. vv. 4–15 below, and Deut. 25. 17–19).

Just as the Amalekites are introduced into the story without explanation, so also are *Joshua* and *Hur*. Hur is mentioned again at 24. 14 as a kind of deputy judge, but we know nothing else of him. Joshua, by contrast, plays an increasingly prominent part in the story, eventually being installed as Moses' successor and leading the people triumphantly into the promised land. The description of the battle is curious; for once divine intervention is not prominent. Instead the picture of Amalek's defeat is presented in virtually magical terms, depending on the ability of Moses to keep his *hands steady*. It would be attractive, but quite lacking in justification from the text, to think that his hands were outstretched in prayer.

17. 14–15   Those who have supposed Moses to be the author of the book we now have have made much of this verse, with the divine instruction to him to *record this in writing*. Presumably he did so, but the fact is not recorded. In any case the point is to emphasize in a solemn way the hostility between Yahweh and Amalek. Not only the writing, but the construction of *an altar* underline the point. The meaning of the next phrase is uncertain, but it is a solemn assertion of the continuing hostility between *the* LORD and *Amalek*.

18. 1–4   We now have a flashback to the story in ch. 2, and more particularly to 3. 1, where Moses' *father-in-law* was called *Jethro priest of Midian*. The name of Moses' wife *Zipporah* and of their elder son *Gershom*, with the explanation of his name, recall 2. 21–22. We have not heard previously, however, of a second child, *Eliezer*. The explanations of the names of the two sons give us a summary of the key themes of Moses' life so far.

18. 5–9   The meeting between Moses and Jethro is now described. It takes place *at the mountain of God*, where Moses had tended his father-in-law's sheep in 3. 1. This develops the link with Horeb mentioned in 17. 6, though the name itself is not here found, and acts as a pointer to the further development from ch. 19 onwards. When he heard Moses' story *Jethro rejoiced*. This can certainly be read simply as a sign of his pleasure that all had gone well, but many interpreters have seen here a pointer to something more significant. It has been suggested that

Jethro's priesthood was actually devoted to Yahweh, and that his rejoicing was related to the power of his God and all that he had done *for Israel's sake*, and *how he had saved them*. The origins of the worship of Yahweh are very obscure, so that we should be unwise to put too much weight on this theory, but it is certainly a possibility.

18. 10–12   If the theory just outlined were to be accepted, these verses could then be seen as supporting it. Jethro offers the blessing; he takes the story of the deliverance *from the power of Egypt and of Pharaoh* as confirming the greatness of the God whom he worships; and he brings *a whole-offering and sacrifices*. It would not have been acceptable to the author of Exodus to have *Aaron and the elders of Israel* sharing a sacred meal with the devotees of other gods.

18. 13–23   Jethro's final contribution to the story is an interesting piece of practical advice. This is one of those episodes which follows the tradition of 12. 37 and envisages the community as being of massive size. There are enough *disputes* among them to keep *Moses* constantly occupied, and the proposed resolution can refer to *units of a thousand*. Parts of the story look as if it is concerned with civil cases between different members of the community, whereas elsewhere it is concerned with the conveying of *the statutes and laws of God*. Historically this would be a problem, because these have not yet been given.

18. 24–27   The most natural explanation of this little episode now emerges. It seems likely that it reflects later judicial practice in Israel, which is here validated by being traced back to, and given the authority of, Moses himself. The *capable men* form a *permanent court*. Jethro then leaves the scene, and, under that name at least, plays no further part in the biblical narrative (though cf. Num. 10. 29, where his alternative name 'Reuel' is once again found.)

The Israelites at Mount Sinai

19. 1–40. 38

The promise of the Covenant
19. 1–19. 25

19. 1–6 We have reached *the third month*. This was the time for the celebration of the Feast of Weeks, according to the festal calendar (Deut. 16. 10; it is called 'Harvest' at Ex. 23. 16). It is possible that our author intended the experience at Mount Sinai to be associated with that feast; certainly later Jewish tradition did so. In a comparable way it is possible that the description in Acts 2 of the events at Pentecost (the Greek name for the same festival) is a claim to the setting aside of the Jewish law by God's Spirit.

The opening verses of this section invite us to ask geographical questions, but as we have seen already, they are in practice unanswerable. In particular the location of *Sinai* remains unknown. A newspaper article appeared as this commentary was being written, describing a claim by a well-known archaeologist that the 'true' Sinai should be sought in the Negev, in the modern state of Israel. An Israeli scholar was reported as commenting, 'There are 25 places where Sinai is supposed to have been. Now we have 26.' The tradition that places the mountain near the Gulf of Sinai is not earlier than the Common Era, and we should admit that any attempt at identification can be no more than guesswork.

More important than speculative geography is the way in which this section forms the prologue to the giving of laws which is to follow. The particular emphasis is on the distinctive status of Israel, God's *special possession*. This is expressed in terms of a *covenant*, a relation which looks both back to Genesis (e.g. Gen. 17. 1–9), and forward to ch. 24, when the covenant is sealed after the giving of the Ten Commandments and the laws in chs 21–23 often referred to as the 'covenant code'. The people are also referred to as a *kingdom of priests*, a theme picked up and reapplied elsewhere in the Hebrew Bible (e.g.

Isa. 61. 6), and in the New Testament (I Peter 2. 9). If it is interpreted as a reference to a priestly status for all members of the community, it is of course somewhat at odds with the stress elsewhere in the Hebrew Bible (including Exodus itself) on the setting apart of those of a particular clan as priests. Alternatively, 'of priests' may be seen as a way of describing the kingdom that is to be established: it is not to be like other kingdoms, but is to have a distinctive religious status.

19. 7–9a   Throughout this chapter God is pictured as inhabiting the top of the mountain, and Moses as mediator between God and people has to make a series of journeys up and down the mountain. We need not take this literally and suppose that it was a cruel way to treat an eighty-year-old man. The older understanding of this material, found in both Jewish and Christian writers, which interpreted Moses' mountain journeys as symbolizing a kind of pilgrimage, is more in sympathy with the text. In this section he goes down, receives a favourable response from the people, and goes back up again. Another symbol of the divine presence is then introduced: *a thick cloud*, from which God will speak to Moses. Unexpectedly the purpose of this visitation is that the people's *faith in* Moses *may never fail*.

19. 9b–16   Now the people are to be prepared for the encounter with God. Various signs of what is required are spelt out. Some may seem very mundane, such as the requirement to *wash their clothes*, though this has its own importance as a way of ensuring purity. The next concern relates to the idea of sacred space. *The mountain* is here pictured as the divine dwelling-place which no ordinary mortal may touch. If someone does touch it, the contagion involved is so great that that person must *be put to death* without being touched by anyone. This sanctity is apparently not a permanent condition, for at a given signal, when *the ram's horn sounds*, the prohibition is withdrawn. One more prohibition remains: *do not go near a woman*. We are forcibly reminded that the first readers or hearers of our text will have been exclusively male, and we encounter the idea that women are somehow unclean, an idea which is distressingly persistent, as opposition to the ordination of women in some parts of Judaism and Christianity shows. It appears as if the prohibition is not simply against sexual intercourse; even to be near a woman was too risky. The section ends by spelling out the characteristic outward signs of the divine presence, what is sometimes called a 'theophany': *thunder, lightning, dense cloud,*

trumpet-blast. It was entirely appropriate that, when confronted with such phenomena, the people *trembled*.

19. 17–25   The solemn preparations for the divine manifestation continue, heightening in intensity. We seem to have moved a long way from v. 6 with its picture of a 'holy nation'. Now it is the *mountain* that is *holy*. Reference is made to *priests*, but this appears to anticipate the requirement to set apart certain members of the Levites as priests in ch. 28. Apart from Jethro in ch. 18, we have not yet heard of any particular individuals being set apart for this role. The chapter ends with *Moses* going down to the people, and we are told that he *spoke to them*; yet what follows does not take any account of that, but begins with words attributed to God. Conventionally this break has been ascribed to the awkward joining of two sources, but this seems un-likely; if one holds to a theory of sources, they have elsewhere been brought together much more skilfully. The discontinuity may be a literary device to heighten the impact of the words which are to follow, but few convincing parallels to the use of such devices have been found. We must admit continuing uncertainty.

The Decalogue
20. 1–20. 21

20. 1–17   There follows what has become one of the best-known sections of the whole Hebrew Bible: the 'Decalogue' or 'Ten Com-mandments'. The days are probably past, at least in Christian circles, when children were required to learn them by heart, but they are still widely called upon, either approvingly, as the rules by which a religious society should govern its behaviour, or, more critically, as typifying the negative nature of religious demands (eight of the commandments feature the word 'not', and of the remaining two, the command to observe the Sabbath can also be considered as essential-ly restrictive). Before we look at the commandments in detail, how-ever, there are some general comments that need to be made about the collection as a whole.

We shall be wise to note, first of all, that, though there is universal agreement that there are ten commandments, there are different ways of enumerating them. The main problem arises in vv. 1–4. The traditional Jewish understanding treats v. 2, 'I am the LORD . . . land of slavery' as the first in the series, whereas all Christian traditions have taken it as preliminary, with v. 3 ('You must have no other god besides me') as the first commandment. But after that the Christian tradition is itself divided. Catholics and Lutherans take v. 4, referring to the 'carved image', as part of the first commandment, whereas other Christian bodies take this to be number two in the series. From then on as far as v. 16 there is no dispute about the extent of each commandment, but the Catholic/Lutheran mode of reference is one lower. This has at times had unexpected consequences. Thus, it was once customary to speak of sexual offences as 'breaking the seventh commandment': meaningful in Reformed or Anglican usage, but quite misleading to Catholics or Lutherans, for whom the seventh commandment referred to theft! The two traditions finally joined in v. 17, treated as a single commandment by most Protestant Christians, but divided into two by Catholics and Lutherans.

Another point of which we should be aware is that the Decalogue is found twice in the biblical text: here, and in Deut. 5. There are minor differences of wording between the two forms, but the only difference of any significance comes in the reason given for Sabbath observance, which we will look at when we reach v. 11.

It would be possible to write a great deal on the later history of interpretation of the Decalogue. Within the Hebrew Bible the fact that it occurs twice may testify to its importance, for laws are not often found twice in such slightly changed form, but otherwise it plays a less prominent part than might have been expected. The stories in the 'historical books' never refer to the Decalogue, even in those cases where it might have seemed directly relevant. Thus David's behaviour toward Bathsheba and her husband Uriah, described in II Sam. 11–12, flouted the commandments against both adultery and murder, but they are not referred to. Similarly the condemnation of those who defrauded Naboth in the matter of his vineyard (I Kings 21) does not allude to the Decalogue. There are no clear references to it in the Prophets; Hosea 4. 1–2 might be interpreted as having the Decalogue as its background, but this is by no means unambiguous, and it would certainly be possible to argue that the final form which we have is actually later than that section of Hosea. It might well be that the prophetic attacks formed the basis for a collection of laws, codifying and structuring that material, though scarcely in the sense of forming it into a law-code. The explanations that are appended to most of the individual commandments might suggest that the Decalogue was regarded as a basis for preaching God's will. Incidentally, the classical Jewish tradition of interpretation does not seem to have regarded the

Decalogue as being in any way of unique importance; there are no special sections devoted to it in Mishnah or Talmud. Later Jewish thought has, however, 'claimed' the Decalogue, perhaps partly as a reaction to the importance it was granted by Christians. One Jewish tradition, for example, sees a conscious parallel between the 'ten words' here and the ten words attributed to God in the first story of creation (Gen. 1. 1–2. 3).

Probably the most important feature of later interpretation, however, is the way in which the commandments have been universalized in Christian tradition. They are addressed to individuals – the 'thou shalt not' of older translations, and as we shall see when we look at the individual requirements, most of them can be given a very specific application within the structure of ancient Israelite society. In contrast to that, much Christian tradition has regarded the commandments as being universally applicable. Their recitation is required, and was for long usual, in the Church of England Book of Common Prayer service of Holy Communion, and they have featured regularly in catechisms and other manuals of instruction aimed at children. The underlying assumption has been that they provide a set of rules which can shape the whole of the believer's life.

One very obvious example of such universalizing is the prohibition on committing adultery (v. 14). As we shall see, that has a very specific (and therefore limited) reference, but it has come to be understood as a prohibition of any sexual behaviour considered inappropriate by a particular Christian body. In a comparable way, the Christian church has taken over the Sabbath commandment, re-applied it as referring to the first day of the week (so that in old-fashioned Christian circles and still occasionally in tabloid newspapers 'the Sabbath' would normally be taken as meaning Sunday), and thereby radically altered its original thrust. It is no part of the task of this commentary to say that such re-appropriation is wrong, but the way in which it has drastically changed the thrust of the individual commandments should be recognized. Our concern will for the most part be with the exploration of the meaning of the commandments in their setting in ancient Israel.

That in turn raises one further question to which we must attend before engaging in more detailed consideration of the individual laws. In their present setting in Exodus it is clear that these commandments are presented as part of the kind of 'foundation charter' which God had presented to the people from their very earliest days. In fact, as we have noted already, it is unlikely that they should be considered as being anything like as ancient as this would imply. Though some scholars have attempted to defend the view that a nucleus of the commandments might go back to Moses, and therefore to a time before Israel was established in Canaan, the picture the commandments give is of a settled rather than a nomadic society. The danger implicit in alien gods makes better sense in a settled context; still more so does the picture of the Sabbath. Crops can be left to grow during a regular day of rest; such a pattern of life is scarcely feasible for wandering herdsmen, with the flocks of milk-producing animals to attend to. (We need to bear in mind also, as has been mentioned more than once in this commentary, that the traditional picture of Israel as originally a nomadic group living outside Palestine is in any case a very doubtful one.)

The lack of reference to the commandments in other parts of the biblical material is a point we have already noted. It is of course dangerous to build much on an argument from silence of this kind, but it seems most likely that the commandments as an established block of laws took shape as the people were finding their feet at the time of the Second Temple and the Persian period. Individual laws may certainly have been older, as will, of course, have been the general ethos embodied in many of them. That is to say, there is no suggestion that such a matter as murder or theft only came to be condemned at that period. But there is no firm evidence of a formally structured body of laws at an earlier time.

One other point should be mentioned, as a warning that ideas among biblical scholars have changed a good deal in recent years. The individual commandments are all in what is sometimes called 'apodeictic' form, that is, they consist of direct commands, mostly in the negative (the traditional 'Thou shalt not'). This is in sharp contrast to the commands we shall be concerned with in chs 21–23, which are nearly all 'conditional', spelling out the conditions involved if a particular offence is to be seen as committed. It used to be supposed that these apodeictic commands were peculiarly Israelite, and that this could be fastened upon as a feature differentiating Israel from other parts of the Ancient Near East. The discovery of additional law-codes, and closer study of material already available, has shown that such differentiation is inappropriate. What we shall notice is that the implications of the commands given here are often spelt out in greater detail in the following chapters.

The collection begins with an affirmation, put into God's mouth, and apparently addressed directly to the whole community without human agency. This is unusual; normally God's message is pictured as being mediated through Moses (and Aaron). The affirmation itself is found frequently in slightly varying forms through much of the Hebrew Bible: *I am the* LORD *your God who brought you out of Egypt, out of the land of slavery*. This is important in several ways. It provides what amounts to a definition of the divine character; it acts as a link between the two parts of the Book of Exodus; it also serves as an important means of self-identification for the group which put the Decalogue together. They are laying claim to possession of the distinctive history of the community. The laws which are to follow through the remainder of the book must be seen in the context of the deliverance from the troubles which the people had experienced in Egypt.

There follows the prohibition of the recognition of any *other god*. It seems fairly clear that in the monarchical period Yahweh had not been the only god worshipped in Israel, and it is not even certain that it was felt essential that he should be. But there emerged what has been described as a 'Yahweh-alone' party, represented in Hosea and the compilers of the book of Deuteronomy, and from then on the community came increasingly to be identified as worshippers of Yahweh and of no other god. We need to bear in mind the transformation that took place; once a nation-state, from the sixth century BCE onwards the community was essentially a religious group bound together by their common worship in the Yahweh-temple at Jerusalem.

This development is further reflected in vv. 4–6. It remains disputed whether Yahweh himself had been represented by any form of imagery in earlier times, but it seems clear that his worship became 'aniconic', that is to say, rejecting any kind of statuary or other imagery. Here any form of such imagery is rejected, the clear implication being that the making of a *carved image* or *likeness* would inevitably lead to false *worship*.

The reason for this is then spelt out in terms of Yahweh being a *jealous God*. The basic meaning here is surely a concern that he, and not foreign gods, should be the object of worship. Commentators have been at pains to stress that the modern negative resonance of the word 'jealous' should not be seen here, and up to a point they may be right. But it would be wrong to protest too much. 'Jealousy' in its negative sense is far from extinct among religious believers, and can certainly be projected also on to the gods whom they worship. Rivalry between gods could be a very serious matter, and the promise of *punishing* those who were disloyal, and *keeping faith* with those *who love me and keep my commandments* is a natural consequence of such rivalry. The threat of *punishing the children for the sins of the parents* can be seen as a fact of life, and it is also true that the world of the Hebrew Bible shows greater solidarity between different generations than is customary in the modern West. Despite all that, the unattractive element embodied in such a threat still remains.

In v. 7 the concern for *the name* is less obvious. Name and identity go closely together, and Deuteronomy and texts thought to have been influenced by Deuteronomy frequently refer to 'the name of the Lord' instead of making direct reference to the Lord himself. The most obvious consequence of this command has been the refusal of Jews to use the divine name. In the Hebrew Bible itself the consonants of the divine name, Y-h-w-h, are provided with the vowels of a different word, *Adonay*, from which the word 'Jehovah' has been formed. This is a made-up English word, first found in Christian usage in the late Middle Ages, and is not found in Jewish usage. Among Jews, incidentally, it is still common to render the word 'God' as 'G-d'.

The Sabbath command, vv. 8–11, brings us to one of the characteristic marks of the community of Judaism. It is one of the features which has led scholars to suggest that the Decalogue was a product of the Second Temple period, for there are very few references to the Sabbath in earlier literature. That the Sabbath was a day to be marked by some form of religious rite is suggested by II Kings 4. 23, but there is no suggestion there of the rest from labour which is so prominent here. Both the Kings text and Amos 8. 5 link Sabbath with New Moon as times of special religious observance, but there is no link with the moon here. Instead, Sabbath is linked with the *six days* of creation described in Gen. 1.1–2. 3, with the clear implication that God had himself observed the Sabbath at the end of his creative activity.

As already noted, this is the one point at which the form of the Decalogue in Exodus differs quite substantially from that found in Deuteronomy 5. 12–15. There the reason for the Sabbath rest might be described as humanitarian, ensuring that everyone received a fair day of rest; here a more specifically theological reason is set out. For those who wish to pursue source criticism this is one reason for classing our present text as 'P' (Priestly), along with Gen. 1.

What our text does share with Deuteronomy is a very specific identification of those being addressed. It is someone who is able to work (and work here is regarded, if not as desirable, then at least as necessary; it is not a curse in the way that it is pictured in Gen. 3.

17–19). The one addressed is clearly male, and a prosperous male at that, able to afford to take a rest, someone with a *slave* and a *slave-girl*, the possessor of *cattle*. He may be expected to have a grown-up family, for *son* and *daughter* are pictured as being capable of working, but no mention is made of a wife. The prominence of women in the early chapters of Exodus has long been forgotten.

To keep the sabbath day holy does not appear to envisage specific acts of worship; all the emphasis is on rest. In practice, with the development of the synagogue, Jews have habitually gathered for worship on the Sabbath, but this is scarcely attested as a regular custom before the Common Era. Both in treating the first day of the week as a 'Sabbath', and in its emphasis on worship, the Christian church has gone a long way from the original concern of this commandment.

With the command to *honour* parents the thrust of the commandments changes. Thus far their prime concern has been with the community's obligations towards its god. From here on fellow human beings come to the fore, as is noted in Eph. 6. 2, where this commandment is referred to among the instructions to different members of early Christian families. The assumption is that the parents to be honoured will be elderly; there is no suggestion that these commandments were addressed to children, though that is another way in which they have often been re-applied in a Christian context. Different readers will no doubt assess differently how far this commandment should be seen as reflecting a genuine and admirable concern for the elderly, and how far it includes a recognition that its framers would one day themselves be elderly and hope to receive equal honour. It may not be too cynical to see this point as underlying the promise of *long life* for those who observe the commandment.

The extreme brevity of the next four commandments (vv. 13–16) has led some scholars to suppose that there was an original form of this block of laws in which all the commands were comparably brief. It may be so, but any such reconstruction has to be speculative; no briefer form has survived. Another way of explaining the difference in length is to suppose that the earlier commands needed explanation and justification, whereas these are self-evidently necessary for the proper functioning of society. But this procedure is not without risks, for the meaning of some of these commands is less obvious than might appear.

Thus, at v. 13, NEB has *Do not commit murder*. Older readers may remember that AV had here 'Thou shalt not kill'. It is obvious that these two translations are quite different in their thrust. We can say straightaway that if the older translation were what was intended the commandment was largely ignored, for there are many killings described and alluded to in both the Hebrew Bible and the New Testament without any suggestion that God's command is being flouted. A more nuanced rendering is clearly needed; the difficulty arises in whether REB (supported also by other modern translations such as NRSV) has got the right nuance. Murder is wrong in all known societies; the problem lies in what is to be so defined. The verb is not the usual one for 'kill'; one suggestion is that what is envisaged here is a limitation on the practice of blood-revenge. This is certainly a concern reflected in the legal material in Exodus as we shall see when we reach 21. 23–25.

Do not commit adultery (v. 14) is another command which needs careful definition. As we have seen already, it has come to be interpreted as a warning against any form of unacceptable sexual behaviour, but something much more specific seems to be implied. These commands are primarily addressed to the male members of the Israelite community. It is taken for granted in different parts of the Hebrew Bible that men had recourse to prostitutes, and that practice, though seen as a dangerous one by the Book of Proverbs, is never specifically condemned. The point here clearly is that adultery means having sex with another man's wife, seen as in effect his possession. To have his property used in this way would bring shame on the other man, with ominous consequences for the well-being of the community. We are still in the world where blood-revenge was a threat, as we saw in the command against murder.

This remains true with the warning *Do not steal*. It is of course true in both the ancient and the modern world that prohibitions of theft come only from those who have property that is worth stealing. As we saw in the introduction to the Decalogue the commandments reflect the concerns of the male propertied classes. But it may be appropriate to see here more than simply a concern to keep one's possessions intact. As with the two preceding commands, there may be an underlying fear of blood-revenge as a likely consequence of theft, as of murder and adultery.

Something similar seems to be true of the prohibition of giving *false evidence*. This is not simply a general warning against telling lies; it is once again more specific: lying when in the witness-box. Again we see an underlying concern for the maintenance of the established order of society. Accusations that justice was no longer being maintained are a common subject of prophetic oracles, and the story of Naboth in I

Kings 21 provides an interesting insight into ways in which justice could be subverted. Perhaps the established classes were right, and any break-up of their order would have led to a descent into anarchy, but it seems clear that these commands also reflect their own proprietorial interest.

The last commandment (last two in the Catholic-Lutheran tradition) is one of the most difficult to interpret. REB follows a long tradition in seeing it as a prohibition of 'coveting' any of one's neighbour's possessions. Here quite specifically his *wife* is listed along with *slave, slave-girl, ox* and *donkey* as that which *belongs to him*. To that extent this commandment is in line with those which have preceded. But is what is prohibited here simply a matter of thought or intention? It is difficult to see how that could be the subject of a law, and those who have seen in the Ten Commandments the basis of a code of laws have supposed that the traditional translation must be wrong. (In the other version of the Decalogue, at Deut. 5. 21, the wife is separated out from the other possessions and a different verb is used [REB: 'lust after'], but that does not appear to help our immediate problem.) The fact is that attempts to suppose that the prohibition here was not just of coveting, but of following that covetousness by some act of wrongful seizure lack any basis in the text. It really does seem as if the thought police are not just a modern invention. In any case the imprecision of this commandment, not least in its reference to *anything* that belongs to the neighbour, may show the beginnings of a process of universalizing the commands. It certainly warns against the supposition that the Decalogue should be understood as a formal set of 'laws'.

20. 18–21   Just as the Decalogue at its beginning seemed to interrupt the flow of the narrative, so it is at the end. In context it is curious that *the people* should say *do not let God speak to us or we shall die*, for the words of the Decalogue have just been addressed to them. These verses serve as a bridge passage between the giving of the commandments and the spelling out of their detailed implications in the next chapters. They form a typical theophany, that is a manifestation of the divine presence. All the signs described here are characteristic of such a divine visitation: *thunder, lightning, the trumpet,* and *the mountain in smoke*. The only appropriate response to God's presence is that the people *were afraid and trembled*. They are reassured; all that has happened is to serve as a *test*.

The Covenant
20. 22–23. 33

20. 22–26 These verses begin a section which extends to the end of ch. 23, and is often described as 'the Book of the Covenant', on the assumption that this material is what is referred to by that name at 24. 7. It has very little connection with the narrative context in chs 19 and 24; there are no references to Sinai, or to the dramatic events which have been described. Some parts of this material are reminiscent of timeless wisdom sayings, but overall this section is usually read as a body of laws, dealing with a variety of themes – mainly but by no means exclusively religious. The present passage begins with a very cursory link to God's having *spoken from heaven* (presumably in the Decalogue), and thereby fulfilling the requirements laid down in 19. 3. The passage then goes on to two apparently unrelated religious concerns. The first is a warning against the construction of *gods of silver* and *gold*. This could be a reference to the 'carved images' of v. 4, but is not elaborated further. Instead the main concern of this section is the second point, not a matter addressed in the Decalogue: the nature of the *altar* at which Yahweh was to be worshipped.

This is clearly regarded as an important matter, for very specific requirements are laid down. It would seem as if these requirements reflect an early stage in the community's growth, for they hardly reflect the practice of a settled group worshipping in a temple. The literary form is one which modern readers may find somewhat puzzling. It seems as if a very specific requirement is laid down: Yahweh's altar must be *of earth*, as if no alternative was permissible. But then in v. 25 an alternative is envisaged: *an altar of stones*. This manner of setting out possibilities is not unusual in the Hebrew Bible (or in later Jewish usage). The passage assumes the offering of *whole-offerings and shared offerings*, though the requirements for these have not yet been set out. Indeed, it is only in the Book of Leviticus that they will be fully expounded. The curious warning against a stepped altar may echo some form of sexual practice now ruled inadmissible; it is scarcely probable at any known historical period that the person offering the sacrifice would be so scantily dressed as to expose himself by accident. (It is striking that there is here no requirement that the offering of sacrifices be confined to priests; though Aaron has frequently been referred to and his priestly status taken for granted, detailed requirements concerning the priesthood will not be set out until ch. 28.)

21. 1   A fresh start is made here. 20. 22–26 is not closely integrated into the following material. This material is customarily referred to as a 'body of laws', though whether that description is appropriate is a question we must consider in a moment. In any case it seems to have little relevance to the supposed historical situation of the community, newly escaped from Egypt as a band of fugitives. We may suppose that the basic thrust here is theological rather than historical. God is pictured as having become the people's God in Egypt and has shown his power in delivering them from oppression. Now he lays down the structures of society which are to govern their life as the people of God. The picture we are given is of a settled people, an agricultural society, concerned with the details of day-to-day life.

There is no possibility of dating this material; such collections represent a long process of gradual accumulation, especially as fresh conditions came to be laid down. Much of the material in these chapters is found also in Deuteronomy. Broadly speaking it seems likely that the form of the 'laws' here is earlier than that found in Deuteronomy, where many individual passages may have undergone significant modification, but it is not possible within the scope of this commentary to make detailed comparisons between the two books.

The difficulty of how best to classify these sayings remains. At first glance they certainly appear to be formulated as laws, often with precise conditions laid down concerning their applicability, as against the universal picture offered in the Decalogue. At the same time it is difficult to envisage how this material could ever have been used in a court of law, and so various proposals have been made: that what we have here should be seen as akin to the wisdom sayings in Proverbs, or more generally a learned tradition concerned to preserve and set down what were regarded as the appropriate modes of behaviour in Israelite society. In the comments that follow individual passages will sometimes for convenience be described as 'laws', but this uncertainty as to their actual function should be borne in mind. We need also to be aware that there are parallels between many of the individual prescriptions and material found in other Ancient Near Eastern law codes. It is not possible in a short commentary like this to spell out these links in detail, but it is important to remember that Israel's life-situation closely resembled that of surrounding cultures.

21. 2   Any thoughts of using Exodus as a key to liberation theology must receive a sharp jolt here. In both Old and New Testaments of the

Christian Bible, the existence of slavery is taken for granted (cf. for example I Peter 2. 18). It has sometimes been argued that the security of life within a settled household meant that slavery was preferable to the uncertainty of life as a free person, but that is very much an upper-class reaction. We rarely hear of anyone choosing slavery, though incentives to do so will be provided in vv. 4–6. Here regulations are set out to govern the practice of purchasing *a Hebrew as a slave*. 'Hebrew' is not a common designation for members of the community in other parts of the Hebrew Bible, and it is possible, though not very likely, that some special group is here envisaged.

21. 3 This verse is the first in a series of conditional (*'If'*) clauses, a characteristic feature of law-codes throughout the Ancient Near East and indeed into modern times. Whereas the unconditional ('apodeictic') laws found in the Ten Commandments laid down broad general requirements, now specific conditions are set out as to the limitations and implications of such laws. Here it is specified that a slave who has completed the six years of service laid down in the previous verse may only take with him the wife he was already married to when the time of service began. Even among slaves there was a hierarchy of genders. There is no legislation relating to the woman in question; she is simply taken for granted.

21. 4–6 Two more conditions are now spelt out. A *woman* might be given to the slave during his time of service. This could have been a prudent move, since a servant with domestic responsibilities was less likely to be a trouble-maker. But when the time of service was up, the woman and her children remained as the master's property; the slave must simply *go away alone*. That provides an obvious cue for the second condition; faced with the prospect of bidding farewell to wife and children, the man might well feel that he was better off where he was, and conclude that *I do not wish to go free*. In that case a formal ceremony was imposed which had the effect of making him a slave *for life*. At *the doorpost* of the house, the slave-owner was to *pierce his ear with an awl*. Whether an ancient equivalent of an earring, making clear whose property the man was, was then inserted, is not made specific. (We should note that in what was probably a later development of the law, in Deut. 15. 12–17, though the provision for ear-piercing remained, a more humane provision with regard to possessions, if not to partners, was laid down.)

21. 7–11   This section provides us with an astonishing insight into the social realities of ancient Israel. It is taken for granted, without comment, that *a man* might *sell his daughter into slavery*! We can only speculate whether this situation was brought about by poverty, perhaps heightened by someone having too many daughters and not enough sons; or whether it was a straightforward sexual deal, making a profit from unwanted girls by selling them to a neighbour's harem. Here in Exodus (again unlike Deuteronomy) a woman in this situation is *to go free*, as male slaves might. Only when her new master found her *unpleasing* was she to be bought back, the literal meaning of *redeemed*. It is not made clear who would be willing or able to buy her back in such circumstances.

Further conditions are then laid down. At least the woman is not to be traded off to *foreigners*, and if she was bought as a gift for the buyer's *son* then she was to have the *rights of a daughter*, such as they were, in her new home. The possibility of a man having more than one wife is here noted without any judgment being passed upon it; the concern of this law is simply to ensure that the less favoured woman is not simply cast aside. The meaning of *meat* and *clothes* is obvious enough; just what the woman's *conjugal rights* may have been is less clear. The word occurs with this sense only here, and, while it is possible that the law expresses a concern for the woman's right to sexual intercourse so that she might become a mother (thus the traditional Jewish interpretation) there is little other sign of such a concern.

21. 12–14   V. 12 introduces us to another form of law. Literally the introduction reads, 'The man who . . .', REB *whoever*. This form will recur frequently in this section (cf. vv. 15, 16, 17). Also characteristic is the form at the end of the verse, translated *must be put to death*. We might almost render the Hebrew as 'the verdict is death'. This expression is found frequently in laws spelling out those crimes which demanded capital punishment.

But whereas v. 12 looks like a reiteration of the commandment in the Decalogue (20. 13), it is followed by conditions which lessen the degree of guilt. The killing may not have been premeditated, but be brought about by what lawyers still call *act of God*. This would at the most be what nowadays would be described as manslaughter, and for those guilty of this offence specific places of refuge would be provided when the people reached Palestine. This is a theme which recurs frequently in later parts of the Hebrew Bible. But the section ends with a warning that if the crime really is murder, then not even God's own altar would provide sanctuary.

21. 15   Violence against one's *father or mother* was particularly heinous. It is not specified whether the striking must have had fatal consequences. Probably not; for in v. 17 we shall see that even to *revile* parents was a capital offence. Here surely the law-maker's thirst for logic has outrun all human considerations, and this is one of several places where we must note but not imitate the laws laid down.

21. 16   *Kidnapping* was also regarded as a capital offence, though again it is very doubtful whether this law was applied in practice. (On 21. 17 see 21. 15 above.)

21. 18–19   If we are to take our cue from the laws, ancient Israel must have been a violent society, for our author's attention now turns to fights which did not lead to the death of the injured party. The law here seems relatively straightforward: provided that the one who is injured recovers sufficiently *to walk about outside*, even if he needs the aid of a *staff*, then the offender is not criminally liable; only *compensation* for *loss of time* is required, together with a not very clear requirement that he *see that his recovery is complete*. The Hebrew Bible is pretty scathing about medical provision (e.g. II Chron. 16. 12), but it may be that there were nurses whose services are here envisaged.

21. 20–21   But if the previous provision seemed comparatively enlightened, we cannot say the same of this. Here *slave* and *slave-girl* (many will prefer the NRSV translation 'male or female slave') are treated simply as pieces of property. Anyone fatally injuring a slave *must be punished*, for the master's property has been damaged. But if the injured person survives, even if only for *one day or two* the threat of punishment is withdrawn. The property has not been instantly made unusable! It is to the credit of Bishop Colenso, mentioned previously in connection with the logistical problems of the story, that he also challenged his readers with the moral problems posed by verses such as this.

21. 22–25   Here further results of violence are brought under consideration. We cannot tell how likely it was that a *pregnant woman* would have been involved in a fracas, but we could envisage circumstances in which she was trying to calm down the violent men. However that

may be, *she has a miscarriage*. If the woman herself suffers no further injury, compensation is payable, but the exact means by which it was determined are not clear: REB here has made the text much more logical than it actually is. The Hebrew text apparently allows the *woman's husband* to lay down the amount of the fine, and the reference to *assessment* is both uncertain in meaning and appears only to be added as a kind of afterthought.

There follows consideration of what is to happen *where injury ensues* to the woman, and this is spelt out in one of the most familiar sets of phrases in the whole Hebrew Bible: *life for life, eye for eye*, and so on. These expressions have often been used as a way of setting out the harshness of Old Testament laws by comparison with the supposedly more merciful attitude to be found in the New Testament, but this is by no means the complete picture. We will not explore here more fully whether the picture thus offered of the New Testament tells the whole story (Matt. 21. 11–14 offers material for reflection), but we should note that an important concern of the lawgiver here is to limit the amount of vengeance that the family of an injured person could claim. A member of their family had been put to shame, and in shame-based cultures this could lead to vendettas that would last over generations. So an important point here is to stress that one life, and only one life, could be demanded where someone had been killed, and proportion-ately where injury had been inflicted. Such an understanding of family relationships may seem primitive in the modern West, but we should remember that Shakespeare's audiences will have been familiar with both the concepts mentioned here: continuing family feuds are illustrated by the Montagues and Capulets in *Romeo and Juliet*; the limitation of the price that could be demanded by the pound of flesh, no more, no less, in *The Merchant of Venice*. In practice, despite these literary allusions, it seems that the injunction was never taken literally in Jewish custom; appropriate monetary compensation was the usual penalty.

21. 26–27   The issue of compensation for injury is now approached from a different angle. We may assume that the *eye* and the *tooth* mentioned here are typical injuries. In such case the *slave*, of either gender, may *go free*. We should assume that slaves so treated would not have been 'devoted to their master' in the way outlined in v. 5.

21. 28–32   The problem of a goring *ox* is dealt with at greater length, suggesting that this was a problem that was liable to recur in an

agricultural society. At first it seems as if the ox is held responsible for its own behaviour, being *put to death* while the owner remained *free from liability*. A number of modifying conditions are then appended. If the dangerous habits of the ox were already known then failure to control it was regarded as a capital offence, and the *owner* was also to be *put to death*. In practice, however, it is most unlikely that such punishment will often have been inflicted. Anyone with enough possessions to own an ox, an expensive animal, will have been a major figure in local society and commutation to a *money payment* will been the usual penalty. It is not specified how the *redemption* payment was assessed; if this passage is taken as a law rather than as a general adage about proper behaviour within society, then we may assume some form of local court that adjudged such matters. The section ends by reminding us that the lives of *slaves* were regarded as relatively expendable.

21. 33–34   Another hazard of agricultural life is here dealt with; the inadequately covered *cistern*. Compensation is here arranged in slightly different form: compensation is to be paid, but the animal's dead body is available to *the owner of the cistern*.

21. 35–36   Now two oxen are involved, in what must have been a sizeable community. Sensible reciprocal arrangements are laid down for the case of 'accidental death', but if the owner of the live beast had failed to heed warnings about his animal's behaviour then the responsibility was his. One can imagine some heated debates in local courts over issues of this kind.

22. 1–4   This section has been reordered in REB, as in other modern translations. If the order preserved in the Hebrew text is correct, its logic is not clear, since it introduces the topic of the thief being killed into the middle of the more general treatment of theft. The commentary here will be based on REB; larger commentaries must be consulted for fuller discussion

First, then, we find a consideration of theft. That theme runs through 22. 1–15, which suggests that this section may be an exposition of the command in the Decalogue against theft (20. 15), just as the previous section was concerned with murder. The law assumes that the detective process which identifies the thief has already taken place, and is concerned with the consequences. The value of *an ox* is once again shown by the requirement of five-fold restitution, which suggests large-scale cattle rustling rather than opportunist thieving. If the convicted thief cannot pay the fine he is condemned to slavery, but if the animal *is found alive* (and presumably in good health) then the fine is reduced to twice its value.

The situation dealt with in vv. 2 and 3a is quite different. Here housebreaking is involved. Anyone doing this during the night is liable to be beaten up by the irate householder; *after sunrise*, however, this is no longer regarded as legitimate defence of one's own property, but is treated as *murder*.

22. 5   The problem here might not at first sight seem to be theft, but it is clearly so regarded by the compiler of this material. A *fire* allowed to *spread* could have devastating effects on a neighbour's property. As in several other passages in this section there is an underlying assumption that an impartial means of assessing damage, *according to the yield expected*, is available.

22. 6   Here again carelessness in allowing a fire to spread is a matter for proper compensation. This is one of the passages where links with the wisdom tradition have been detected, for fire spreading in a *thorn hedge* seems to have been something of a proverbial saying; cf. Ps. 118. 12, where the word 'brushwood' in REB is the same as that here translated 'thorn hedge'.

22. 7–9   More complicated circumstances, with a series of conditions, are now discussed. Valuables are lent *for safe keeping*; there were of course no deposit-boxes or the like in ancient Israel. If they were *stolen* and the *thief apprehended* then a fine was payable as compensation and all was well. But if *the thief was not apprehended* how could one be sure that the goods had actually been stolen? At first it seems as if only the one with whom the goods were deposited had to appear as a witness, but v. 8 extends this by saying that in the matter of any *lost property* both the owner and the one with whom it was deposited had to *appear before God*. 'God' here has often been thought to be a reference to human judges, acting as God's earthly vicegerents (thus NRSV margin). Certainty is impossible, but some form of ordeal, or a solemn oath, may have been required.

22. 10–13   Though animals were mentioned in the previous passage, this appears to be the main body of material concerned with the safe keeping of livestock, which will have been a major issue in a commu-

nity of small agriculturalists. Various circumstances are outlined, all with the underlying assumption that there was *no witness*. Here it is specified that an oath is to be taken, and the divine name is mentioned (*by the* LORD) as against the more general 'before God' of vv. 7–9. This judicial procedure is meant to establish whether or not a theft has taken place and *restitution* is required. But no one could ensure that the loaned animal would not be *mauled by a wild beast*. Provided that there was *evidence* of this fate, no restitution was called for. Amos 3. 12 probably had the fate of the unfortunate animal in mind in its comparison with the impending fate of Samaria.

22. 14–15   The final conditions for a borrowed animal are laid down. One can imagine heated arguments as to what constituted the *owner's presence* in the event of an accident.

22. 16–17   The subject changes abruptly. Those who see in this block of material a spelling out of the implications of the Ten Commandments maintain that the break marks a shift from consideration of the prohibition of theft to that of adultery. That is possible, but not very likely; the offences here condemned cannot be regarded as adultery, which concerns sexual relations with another man's wife. In this first law the issue is the seduction of a young girl. If the man has simply anticipated his forthcoming marriage then he pays *the bride-price* and she becomes his wife. But the girl's father has the right to refuse the union. Of the young woman's wishes and feelings nothing is said!

22. 18   The consequences of this law through much of Christian history have been appalling. Until comparatively recent times it has been possible for men, or for jealous or suspicious women, to declare that someone was a *witch*, and the death penalty was only too likely to be inflicted. No definition of what kind of behaviour characterized a witch is offered.

22. 19   Next bestiality is condemned. As in the modern world, so in the ancient world, it is difficult to know how widespread this practice was. It is not the kind of thing much discussed in polite society, either ancient or modern.

22. 20   Another abrupt change of subject follows. The largest of modern commentaries simply lumps the following material together

as 'Miscellaneous'. Older translations brought this out more clearly by differentiating between second-person singular ('Thou') and second-person plural ('Ye') passages, but that difference is obscured in modern translations. Nor is the original reason for such differentiation clear: a literary device for emphasis? different sources? – various proposals have been put forward for this phenomenon, which is found very frequently in Deuteronomy. The differences will not be spelt out here.

Some of what follows will be attractive to modern readers, other parts very much less so. This verse reminds us how fiercely religious requirements were imposed. Presumably the worshippers of Yahweh were confronted with claims made on behalf of rival deities, and tried to impose their own rules, *under solemn ban*, that is, involving the complete destruction of the one condemned. Readers may not need to be reminded that there is no lack of this kind of religious intolerance in the modern world.

22. 21   A much more attractive picture emerges from this verse. The status of the *alien* in Israel was ambiguous (cf. the last part of Ex. 12, and the discussion there), but at its best the tradition recognized that the story of the people's origin as *aliens in Egypt* demanded generous treatment of other aliens.

22. 22–24   Another important demand for social justice is here laid down. As in many societies *widows* and orphans, perhaps especially those deprived of their fathers, were vulnerable. The dangers to which they were exposed might provide the basis for whole stories; for example, the Book of Ruth. Probably the endings were often less happy than in that tale. It is not clear what means were laid down for them to *appeal to* God. It may have been some form of human judicial appeal, but it seems more likely that, as with the prophets, the law-giver was convinced that God would answer the prayers of the just. We might suppose that the cure was as drastic as the disease, with some killed and more made into *widows and fatherless*.

22. 25   Here is a law which has caused enormous discussion in subsequent ages, for it bans the exacting of *interest* on a loan. In practice, of course, one of the traditional perceptions of Jews in the Christian West has been as *moneylenders*. The law itself limits the prohibition to exacting interest from *any poor man*, and its concern is with *my people*. That definition could be narrowly applied; other parts of the Hebrew

Bible emphasize that all of humanity are God's people, but here that description is confined to the community gathered at Mount Sinai and their descendants.

22. 26–27 Concern for the disadvantaged is found again here. Jesus is pictured in the Gospels as warning his followers against having two coats (Mark 6. 9), and it seems clear that a poor man would simply *wrap* his *cloak* around him at night. It is often supposed that Amos 2. 8 is condemning the failure to take this precept seriously. Striking also is the fact that though this, like the other laws, was addressed to those who were comparatively well-to-do, they were to remember that the poor was still their *neighbour*. As at v. 23 it is not clear whether the *appeal* to God was through a formal judicial procedure or by prayer.

22. 28 We return to the direct command form of law comparable to that found in the Ten Commandments, for a very clear example of the way in which the law was shaped by the ruling classes. In a religious context, all would agree that to *revile God* (suddenly referred to in the third person, though he was notionally the speaker) was deplorable. Here it is put on a par with *cursing a chief of your own people*. The word 'chief' is very unspecific, and cannot be linked with any particular period of the people's history. Essentially the message is to respect those who claim authority.

22. 29–30 The greater part of this little section is straightforward. It was an established practice in ancient Israel, and probably more generally in the Ancient Near East, that firstfruits were to be dedicated to God. Such is the complexity and international inter-dependence of modern agricultural practice that Christian 'harvest festival' services bear little relation to the actual carrying out of a local harvest, but until comparatively recent times the custom of 'Lammas' (='Loaf Mass') maintained the offering of firstfruits. It was extended in Israel to the offering of the firstborn of *oxen and sheep* – a consider-able demand in the case of oxen, but again apparently established practice.

Within these requirements we find the very unexpected demand: *You must give me your firstborn sons*. The natural understanding of this law would be that human sacrifice was to be practised, but both the Hebrew Bible as a whole and laws in other parts of Exodus (e.g. 34. 20) make it clear that this was not the case. How this passage was origin-ally understood we cannot now tell; in its context within the Book of

Exodus, we are invited to recall that Israel was described as God's firstborn (4. 22) and thereby dedicated to God, and that the firstborn of the disobedient Egyptians had been killed (ch. 12).

22. 31   The point just made is emphasized by the beginning of this verse, picturing Israel as *holy* (dedicated) to God. The tone may seem to us to be somewhat lowered by the way this holiness is illustrated – food laws could not readily be applied to what was *killed by beasts in the open country*. That was fit only for the pariah *dogs*. We are a long way from the privations endured by the people in Egypt; now they could be choosy about what they ate.

23. 1   The series of direct divine commands continues, thus maintaining the impression that we are concerned with a body of laws laid down by God. In practice it is not easy to see how a code of laws could legislate against *spreading a baseless rumour*. Honesty in giving *evidence* was and of course still is an essential requirement of a fair legal system.

23. 2–3   The point about honesty in giving evidence is reinforced by a warning against going with *the majority*. Less clear is whether the final warning was needed in practice. Was there a risk that people would be tempted to *show favouritism to a poor person*? History does not supply many examples of this tendency. At the very least this injunction must be read along with v. 6. The REB translation 'poor person' is a little unexpected; the following phrase *his lawsuit* makes clear that only males are envisaged, and this is true of all the laws relating to the poor in this section.

23. 4–5   Though framed as laws, a number of passages in chs 21–23 are difficult to see purely in those terms. We might envisage a law requiring that those who found an *ox or donkey straying* or *helpless under its load* be required to take appropriate action, though such a law would be very difficult to enforce. But to specify that the animals should be those of *your enemy* or *someone who hates you* moves this from a legal requirement to a moral appeal.

23. 6–8   This moral tone is continued in this section. We have noted already the tension between v. 6 and v. 3. Next it is acknowledged that the legal system is not flawless: *lies* may lead to the *death of the innocent and guiltless*. Nothing is said of their being delivered (the Hebrew

Bible for the most part shows little interest in any possible 'future life'), but unspecified divine sanctions are promised against *the guilty*. The dangers to an impartial legal system inherent in *bribery* are then acknowledged.

23. 9 is identical in sentiment and very close in wording to 22. 21. The two verses form an 'inclusio', marking the beginning and end of a distinct section which, as we have noted, is as much moral as legal in its contents.

23. 10–11   This passage at first looks as if it refers simply to agri-cultural practice, warning that it was important for the land to *lie fallow* to restore its productivity. But there are already indications here that the concern is not simply practical, for during the fallow year the *poor of your people* are somehow to be fed – the means is not made clear – and this provision is extended to *vineyard and olive grove*. There was no question of them benefitting from a fallow year! Elsewhere in the Pentateuch, notably in Lev. 25, this 'social concern' expressed through the way in which the land was treated, is developed much more fully. It has led to contemporary calls for a 'Jubilee Year'.

23. 12   The command for abstinence from work on the Sabbath is of course one of the Ten Commandments, but whereas in 20. 8–11 the rationale was God's resting on the seventh day from the work of creation, here, as in the form of the Commandments found in Deuteronomy, concern for *ox and donkey, home-born slave and alien* is the central concern. Deut. 5. 12–15 also has the women of the house-hold in mind; no mention of them here!

23. 13   Again we pass from law to moral exhortation. The Lord is here envisaged as a kind of preacher, and a constant concern of preachers is that people should be *attentive*. The warning against any link with *other gods* is repeated, suggesting that this was a real cause for anxiety at the time that these laws were formed.

23. 14–17   The Pentateuch contains several passages spelling out the annual liturgical pattern laid down for the people's worship; for example, Lev. 23 and Deut. 16 offer much fuller exposition of what is set out briefly here. The three great observances are described as *pilgrim-feasts*, and that is understood to mean the assembling of *all* the adult *males* of the community in one place. Eventually in the light of

Deuteronomy's demand for a central sanctuary that place would be taken to be Jerusalem, but here no place is specified.

The first festival, in the spring *month of Abib* (cf. 13. 4), is here called *Unleavened Bread*, and 'Passover' language is not used. It is possible that the use of the old month name (the later name was 'Nisan'), and the failure to mention Passover means that this law is a relic of older, purely agricultural, usage, but it is noteworthy that the link with the deliverance from *Egypt* is already made. There is an obvious tension between the picture of each of these festivals here as being observed centrally and by males only, and the more domestic picture of Passover set out in ch. 12.

The remaining two feasts are both concerned with harvest; the first, here called simply *the pilgrim-feast of Harvest*, came to be known as 'Weeks', and is concerned with *firstfruits*; the second, in the Autumn, is *Ingathering*, when the harvest was completed. This festival is also called 'Booths' or 'Tabernacles' and was for a long time the most important annual festival. The brevity of the description here might imply that this list was a survival of an early period in the people's history, though they are already pictured as a religious grouping whose males are to make a formal gathering *in the presence of the Lord GOD*. (Here as on several occasions in this material the literary convention that these are God's own words is overlooked.)

23. 18–19   The requirements here form a kind of addendum to the worship pattern just laid down. They are rather miscellaneous and are best treated together. The first requirement is repeated at 34. 25, and seems to be particularly concerned with the feast of Unleavened Bread. Clearly both what was *leavened* and *the fat* produced by the *festal offering* were regarded as having acquired particular sacral associations, which made them dangerous for common use. The requirement that *the choicest firstfruits* be dedicated to God is found several times (e.g. 22. 29); to retain such choice material for personal use was presumably a temptation which those who laid down religious laws felt that they must warn against. More unexpected is the reference to *the house of the LORD your God*, presumably a reference to the Jerusalem temple, and an indication that these laws were formulated at a period much later than that set out in their present context. For different reasons that is illustrated also by the mysterious command not to *boil a kid in its mother's milk*. This requirement is found again at 34. 26 and at Deut. 14. 21, and the after-effects of this law are easy to see: the lay-out of kosher Jewish kitchens to this day requires

the separate preparation of milk foods and flesh meat. Much less obvious are the antecedents of this law, or the reason for it. In the days when anything deplorable, or not properly understood, in ancient Israel's religious practice was blamed on the Canaanites, scholars dismissed this as a Canaanite practice which Israel had for some reason taken over . But there is no convincing evidence from Canaanite texts to support this view. We can only say that by the time that our laws reached their final formulation this had simply become a thing that was 'not done', without any real understanding why it should be so. No reasons for this prohibition are found.

23. 20–26   The body of legal or axiomatic material which began at 20. 22 is now complete, and is followed by a short exhortatory passage of the kind more characteristic of Deuteronomy. It is very general in character, having little to do with the laws and other maxims which have preceded it. The reference to *an angel* may bring to our mind the winged creatures which became an important part of Jewish and early Christian belief around the turn of the eras. A more prosaic understanding seems appropriate here: 'messenger', or the like. It has often been supposed that the reference was to Moses himself, but that can only be speculation. More likely are the suggestions that either this is an oblique way of referring to God's own presence with his people, if they remain obedient, or that the reference is to a succession of divine messengers such as the prophets.

V. 23 sets before us an awful example of a subject that has come much to the fore in recent years: what is now conventionally called 'ethnic cleansing'. Just as unattractive is the name often given to this process in discussion of the Hebrew Bible: 'holy war'. The six nations are the same as those listed in 3. 8, 17, but whereas there the emphasis was on the delights of the land, which was 'flowing with milk and honey', here the human implications are spelt out more radically. To possess that land means to *make an end of* its present inhabitants. Elsewhere those inhabitants are pictured as engaging in all kinds of wrong practice; here, though their worship is of course different, involving other *gods* with *images* and *sacred pillars*, no moral judgment is passed upon these people. This passage is one of several in our book warning of the dangers of human beings creating a god in their own image, convinced that he shares and indeed offers encouragement to their own prejudices. It is disappointing that passages of this kind (and Deuteronomy can be even more blood-thirsty) are not more often the subject of serious reflection among Jews and Christians.

The end of the passage sets out another dangerous misunderstanding too often found among religious believers. If the community are loyal in *worship* then they may expect food and *water*, no *sickness*, no *miscarriages* or *barrenness*, and a *full span of life*. Once again hope triumphs over experience.

23. 27–33   The characteristics of 'holy war' are now spelt out in more detail. *Terror* and *panic* are regular features of such descriptions; this makes it clear that this is no ordinary war decided by the larger numbers or superior fighting skills of one side. In the midst of this vivid language an almost comically practical note is struck. The existing inhabitants are indeed to be driven out, but not too quickly, lest *the land become waste* and *wild beasts* take over. Every eventuality is covered! Equally idealistic is the extent of the land to be captured. Its southern extent is unclear, because, as in earlier references, what is here called *the Red Sea* is 'the Sea of Reeds', whose identity is uncertain. But it is to reach to *the sea of the Philistines*, an unusual description of the Mediterranean, to *the wilderness* on the East, and – somewhat improbably – as far North as the upper reaches of *the river Euphrates*. The passage ends with another warning against any links with the land's inhabitants. They are not even to be allowed to *stay in your* (!) *land*, because of the religious threat they would pose. Anyone wishing to understand the depth of feeling underlying contemporary Middle Eastern politics must be aware of passages like this.

The Covenant accepted
24. 1–24. 18

24. 1–2   The laws and maxims following the Ten Commandments gave us a picture of a society of small agriculturalists. In itself this material bore little relation to their supposed setting at the foot of Mount Sinai, but that context now becomes prominent once more. Ch. 24 as a whole spells out, in sometimes rather confusing fashion, the ratification of the covenant made between God and the community. In this first section *the LORD* is envisaged as dwelling at the top of the mountain, and human access to him is strictly graded. The highest rank is accorded to *Moses*, who *is to approach the LORD by himself*. Next come *Aaron*, two of his sons and *seventy of the elders*. They are to *bow down* in worship at an appropriate distance. Finally *the people* as a whole are not to *go up* the mountain at all. This structuring is remin-

iscent of the gradations in the Jerusalem temple, with God dwelling in the innermost sanctuary, and with rules, worked out no doubt by the priesthood, laying down boundaries beyond which particular groups might not pass.

It is striking that *Nadab and Abihu* are the two sons of Aaron singled out here. They are regularly included in the genealogies (e.g. 6. 23), but the only other occasion on which they are mentioned specifically is a condemnation of their priestly activity (Lev. 10. 1–2). We may discern the rivalry of different priestly groups behind these different stories.

24. 3–8   *Moses'* ascent is deferred until v. 9. Before that he is pictured in a frenzy of activity with the people. First he *repeated to the people all the words of the* LORD; presumably we are meant to envisage that as the contents of chs 20–23. This is a kind of liturgical ceremony to which the people make the appropriate response, *We will do everything.* Next Moses *wrote down all the laws*; then he *built an altar*; then *erected twelve sacred pillars.* This is a somewhat unexpected activity, for pillars are normally associated with the religious rites of those condemned (e.g. 23. 24). Moses' action is however in line with that of the patriarchs whose pillar-raising seems to be approved (e.g. Jacob at Bethel, Gen. 28. 18). These pillars are to symbolize *the twelve tribes of Israel.* This is the first mention in Exodus of such a structured organization (though cf. Gen. 49. 28), and comes to be one way of describing the community. It is favoured by the book of Deuteronomy. It is an idealistic description, looking back from a later perspective; despite attempts to reconstruct a time when Israel was a tribal confederation (the word 'amphictyony' was once a widely used description) there is no historical or archaeological evidence to support such a reconstruction.

Moses' next activity is to have *whole-offerings and shared-offerings*, no doubt of the kind envisaged in Leviticus, made ready. The two types of offering are carefully distinguished in Leviticus; here it seems that the emphasis is simply on the extent of the preparations. Elaborate liturgical specifications follow. *Half the blood* is *flung* against the newly constructed altar; then we hear for the first time of a *Book of the Covenant*, presumably incorporating the material which has been set out in the preceding chapters. As in v. 3, an appropriate response is provided for the people: *We shall obey, and do all that the* LORD *has said.* Finally in this section the remainder of the *blood*, which had been put in *basins*, is *flung over the people*, and said to be *the blood of the covenant* in accordance with all that has been laid down.

This episode is clearly presented as one of great significance in the establishment of the community. It is not difficult to envisage practical problems in carrying out such a ceremony: blood is not easily 'flung'; how many people were involved? (remember that one tradition speaks of some two million people being involved, 12. 37); and a very considerable length of time would have been needed for all the operations described. We are clearly intended to stress the symbolic nature of this ceremony.

24. 9–14   These verses bring us back to the picture in vv. 1–2. The actions there laid down are carried out by the various participants, *and they saw the God of Israel*. This is an astonishing statement, an impossibility according to 33. 20, and to the main body of later Jewish tradition. Indeed it seems as if our author can hardly believe it himself. Though *they saw God, they ate and they drank*, yet *the LORD did not stretch out his hand against the elders of Israel*. The picture of the pavement of sapphire seems to be almost an afterthought, as if at one point this might be presented as symbolic of God's own presence, but the idea is not developed.

Vv. 12–14 are presented in REB as continuous with what has preceded, but they seem to represent a different tradition, and NRSV is probably wise to print these verses as a separate paragraph. Here Moses is told to *come up* (thus repeating v. 9). The *stone tablets with the law and commandments* seem to be an equivalent of the 'Book of the Covenant' of v. 7. Here God does the writing, as against the efforts of Moses in v. 4, and Moses is accompanied by *Joshua his assistant* rather than by Aaron and his sons as in vv. 1, 9. The mention of Joshua in the same context as *Aaron and Hur* reminds us of 17. 8–15, the battle against Amalek. Traditionally these inconsistencies within the narrative structure have been taken as evidence of different 'sources'. That may indeed be so, since it is unlikely that we should regard Exodus as continuous free composition; its author(s) must have had material available to them. But it has been consciously incorporated within the complete story; the repetitions may be illogical when scrutinized in detail, but they give a powerful impression of a climax in the people's progress here being reached.

24. 15–18   Again we have a picture of God's presence, strikingly different from what has preceded. Here *Moses went up the mountain* alone. The *cloud* is not just a meteorological phenomenon, but an indication of the divine presence, and that is brought out more specifically

with a reference to *the glory of the* LORD. This is a mode of expression found especially in Ezekiel (e.g. 1. 28), but whereas there the Jerusalem temple was the proper dwelling -place of that glory, here it *rested on Mount Sinai*, the mountain being mentioned by name for the first time since ch. 19. The specific reference has the effect of drawing chs 19–24 into one 'Mount Sinai' unit. The people are aware of the divine manifestation, which to them *looked like a devouring fire*, but Moses is allowed even to *enter the cloud*. Yet again he *went up the mountain*, but this is repetition for dramatic effect rather than literal description of a series of journeys. We also have here two significant numbers; Moses' entry took place on *the seventh day*. As God had rested on the seventh day after the six days of creation, so Moses is here given a foretaste of the divine rest. And his sojourn on the mountain was to last *forty days and forty nights*, another period of great symbolic significance, taken up, for example, by the Gospel writers in describing Jesus' temptation (Matt. 4. 2). It is also to have a practical significance in our story, for the people regarded it as too long a stay, and unfortunate consequences follow (32. 1).

Instructions for building the sanctuary
25. 1–31. 18

It is dangerous to generalize, but it is likely that for many readers these chapters, and the substantial repetition of much of them in 35–40, will seem to be the most alien part of the book of Exodus. The vivid story of the early chapters can certainly engage us; the Ten Commandments have played a crucial part in shaping moral perceptions in Judaism and Christianity; many even of the more detailed specifications set out in chs 21–23, whether or not we accept their picture of society, at least deal with issues that affect our daily living. But the precise ritual requirements of the chapters we have now reached seem to have little to do with us. Even those who are most punctilious in religious observance in the twenty-first century CE are unlikely to shape that observance by what is laid down here. Already at the beginning of our era the Letter to the Hebrews in the New Testament, and in a much more systematic way the contemporary Jewish writer Philo, were treating this material allegorically rather than literally. That is to say, they saw the requirements spelt out here as standing for the renunciation of different wrong practices and the taking on of good ones. Such an approach cannot be pursued in detail here, partly because of my own lack of expertise, partly because we have become so used to a more literal understanding of ancient texts.

The main interest in these chapters must arise from the way in which a religious community saw its priorities and laid down requirements as to how they were to be carried out. There can be no doubt that the kind of community envisaged in these chapters is radically different from the agriculturalists whose concerns we have found expressed in chs 21–23. Now religious issues, in the sense of matters relating to sacrifice and its proper observance, have become crucial. In theory we are still at Mount Sinai, but it soon becomes apparent that the concerns expressed here are those of the Jerusalem temple, and specifically of its priesthood at a much later period. As noted in the Introduction, source criticism is not a primary concern of this commentary, but the verdict of the source critics that these chapters should be ascribed to 'P', the priestly source, is certainly one that we can accept.

One other characteristic of these chapters may be noted. In no way can they be regarded as poetry, yet they share some of the rhetorical characteristics which we associate with the poetry of the Hebrew Bible. There is much repetition, with subtle differences of wording, both in the individual components of these chapters and in the way in which their substance is repeated in chs 35–40. The section as a whole can be said to build up to a climax, the material preparation of the holy place leading up to the spelling out of the human requirements of its service. It remains an alien world, but we can perhaps see something of the literary skill which portrays that world.

25. 1–7   A first requirement of a religious centre is the generosity of those who participate in its worship. Forgotten is the desperate poverty of the escape from Egypt; now the community is pictured as being able to provide *contributions* of every kind. Older commentators ingeniously supposed that this material abundance came from 'the spoiling of the Egyptians' (12. 35–36); moderns more prosaically but more realistically take it that we have moved here to a different story framework. The meaning of some of the contributions listed as acceptable is disputed, and illustrate a particular difficulty for translators. REB *dugong-hides*, for example, is taken over from NEB 'porpoise', which was accompanied by the charming footnote 'strictly *sea-cow*'. Not many readers will be familiar with the 'dugong', defined in the Shorter Oxford English Dictionary as 'a large herbivorous mammal of the Indian seas'. Apart from the question whether the identification is correct, the question is raised whether the aim of translators should be the greatest degree of biological accuracy, or the provision of something which readers may be expected to understand. NRSV is perhaps on safer ground with its reference to 'fine leather'. In any case such a high-quality imported skin seems scarcely appropriate for a fugitive community at Mount Sinai. The emphasis already is upon only the highest quality of material being appropriate for the service of God.

25. 8–16 A tension emerges in these verses which runs through much of the subsequent description. On the one hand we have the command, *Make me a sanctuary*, the clear implication being that a fixed place of worship is envisaged. It is taken for granted that God will *dwell among the Israelites* in the sanctuary. Here the special status of the Jerusalem temple seems clearly to be envisaged. But the next word used is more ambiguous. The word 'dwell' (Heb. *shakan*) forms the basis of the word translated *Tabernacle* (*mishkan*), and thus reinforces the idea of a fixed dwelling-place. But the tabernacle is also pictured as if it were a movable structure, a kind of elaborate tent. One solution of the problem is along source-critical lines: that one source spoke of a fixed tabernacle, another of a portable 'tent of meeting', but that raises the problem of an apparently very careless final editor who failed to spot the inconsistency. It may be better to recognize the differences as lying in the very basic human desire to picture God both as associated with particular holy places and as present in every aspect of a community's life.

A further complication is introduced by reference to an *Ark*. This is the first reference to what will come to be known as 'the ark of the covenant'. We need first of all to bear in mind that the word here used for 'ark' has no relation to that used of Noah's 'ark', which was also used of the 'rush-basket' in which the infant Moses was placed at 2. 3. What is now described is a small container; we cannot be precise as to its measurements, as different *cubits* are found in the Hebrew Bible, but we can think of a vessel somewhat more than a metre in length and approximately 70 cm in breadth and height. There are frequent references to an ark in many parts of the Hebrew Bible. Here we must confine ourselves to the account given in Exodus.

The esteem in which the ark was to be held is indicated by the insistence that everything was to be covered with *gold*. *Poles* for carrying the ark, with *rings*, all of gold or with gold overlay, were required; when complete the ark was to have within it *the Testimony*. Apart from an anticipatory allusion in 16. 34, this is a new term, which would give rise to one of the descriptions of the ark ('the Ark of the Testimony', v. 22). It appears in effect to be synonymous with 'covenant' (NEB and NRSV actually translate with 'covenant' here); if a difference of emphasis was intended we no longer know what it was, but in the present shape of the book we are to assume that the testimony contained the words of God referred to in ch. 24.

25. 17–22   The measurements of the *cover* show us that the ark was not completely enclosed. Instead the *ends of the cover* were to contain *two gold cherubim*. This is a word which has changed its meaning very drastically. Nowadays cherubs may bring to our mind charming little figures from Renaissance paintings. In the Hebrew Bible, however, from their first introduction at the forbidden entrance of the Garden of Eden (Gen. 3. 24) they were creatures whose function was to protect the sacred from profane interference. Our passage thus provides a link backward to the account of creation and forward to the cherubim in the Jerusalem temple (I Kings 6. 23–28). The question whether they might constitute a 'carved image', and thus be in contravention of the Ten Commandments (20. 4) seems not to have been a concern of the author.

25. 23–30   Further details of the furnishing of the sanctuary are now provided. The *table* is somewhat smaller in dimensions than the ark, but is similarly to be overlaid with *gold*, as are the carrying-poles. Even the various vessels required – *dishes and saucers, flagons and bowls* – are all to be of *pure gold*. Ostentation rather than practicality seems to be the order of the day. The section ends with a passing reference to *the Bread of the Presence*. This is the 'shewbread' of older versions; here its existence is taken for granted, though not until Leviticus 24 is the method of preparation and its significance as a symbol of the covenant spelt out. If there had once been any suggestion that the reason for placing the bread in the sanctuary was in case the god needed food, that thought has been quite overlaid here.

25. 31–40   Next to be described is the *lampstand*, with its *six branches*. Such furnishings were of course an essential part of holy buildings, both the tabernacle described here and the various temples built in honour of the gods. But they also came to have important symbolic significance, typically expressed by the letters to the seven churches in the Book of Revelation (e.g. 1. 12–13). In Jewish tradition, too, the

m^e*norah*, the seven-branched candlestick, has been of great symbolic importance right down to the present day and its use by the modern state of Israel. As with much of the description of the tabernacle and its furnishings, it is impossible to be certain whether actual objects, known to at least the priestly classes, are being described, or whether much here is intended as symbolic.

26. 1–6   The literary character of the description is now well illustrated. If this were merely a prosaic account of architectural features, we should expect the building to be described first, and then its contents. Here, however, the order is reversed. We have already been told of ark, table and lampstand before we come to an account of *the Tabernacle itself*. But once again we have to be patient. Instead of an account of the building, we have first a description of its *hangings*. These are 'curtains' in most translations; however translated, the concern that the divine presence should be enclosed is an important one, and this chapter and the next will have many references to such hangings, various Hebrew words being employed. The author and no doubt most readers of this commentary spend their lives in walled buildings, but tents with – often elaborate – hangings played an important part in the life of ancient Israel. They do not imply nomadism, but even settled agriculturalists needed tents when shepherding flocks, and the picture of God as a shepherd ties in very readily with the picture of his dwelling in the very best kind of tent. The reference to *cherubim* as now no more than decorative features of the hangings suggests that their protective function (cf. 25. 18–22) has given place to something which is purely ornamental.

26. 7–14   The precious hangings around the ark are themselves enclosed within more functional *hangings of goats' hair*, to form an exterior *tent*, exposed to the elements. The violet loops and gold fasteners of the tabernacle itself are replaced here by *loops* of unspecified material and *bronze fasteners*. These requirements reflect a mixture of practical concern, less precious material being more appropriate for exterior use, and an awareness of greater distance from the presence of the deity.

26. 15–25   Now we move back to the *uprights* which are to support the actual *Tabernacle*. To describe any architectural construction in words, without the use of pictures or diagrams, remains an extremely difficult task, and we cannot be sure that all the details have been

conveyed accurately. The word translated *frames* occurs frequently from v. 15 on, but its exact meaning is uncertain: 'boards' and 'planks' have also been suggested. Those who wish to pursue this topic further must explore the various Bible dictionaries; the only two general points that emerge are the concern for symmetricality, expressed by phrases like *Do the same* and *both alike*, and the fact that even the frames are lavishly decorated, with *silver sockets*.

26. 26–30 In the midst of further technical description we have one of the few conscious attempts to set this block of material in its larger setting. All is to be done in accordance with the *design you* (Moses) *were shown on the mountain*. No specific reference seems to be intended; this is simply a way of reminding the reader that the community is still to be pictured as gathered around Mount Sinai.

26. 31–35 The word here translated *curtain* is different from that rendered 'hanging' earlier in the chapter, but is apparently synonymous with it. The older translations (e.g. AV) brought out the sense with their rendering 'veil'; the divine presence was to be veiled from unauthorized eyes. It was this 'veil' in the Jerusalem temple which the Gospel writers picture as 'torn in two from top to bottom' (Mark 15. 38), as the death of Jesus symbolized the breaking-down of barriers between divine and human.

The existence of such divisions is emphasized by the first command within this section which requires action. The *ark of the testimony* is to be brought *inside the curtain*, and the point, implied several times previously, is now made explicit: there is to be a *clear separation*. The distinction *between the Holy Place and the Holy of Holies* is strongly reminiscent of the various parts of the Jerusalem temple, all of which was a 'holy place', but a particular part was distinguished as being the 'Holy of Holies'.

26. 36–37 One requirement remains for this section. The *tent* itself must have a *screen*, which will have the negative purpose of keeping out intruders but must also be finely decorated because of its privileged position.

27. 1–8 We come next to *the altar*, and are confronted at once with an obvious practical difficulty. How could a construction of *acacia-wood* be appropriate for use as an altar on which burnt sacrifices were to be offered? Even the *bronze overlay* would be totally inadequate. Clearly

the author has in mind the fact that he is describing a portable sanctuary (v. 7), and in that regard the small size of this altar and its wooden construction would have been appropriate, as against the usual stone-constructed altar. Despite the elaborate requirements for disposing of *fat and ashes* in this section, the altar can never have been used for sacrifice. It is a purely literary edifice.

In one other detail the usual construction of altars is to be observed: the provision of *horns at the four corners*. Their purpose may have been practical, the protuberances helping to secure the body of the sacrificial animals, but they came also to have symbolic significance, as a place of sanctuary. David's general Joab is said to have backed the losing side in Solomon's *coup d'état*, and he 'laid hold of the horns of the altar' (I Kings 2. 28), but this was not enough to save him from Solomon's vengeance (vv. 31–34). Our present section ends with another reminder that the immediate context was what was *shown* to Moses *on the mountain*.

27. 9–19   If the requirement for a wooden altar arose from the practical concern for its portability, that issue seems now to be overlooked, for the *tabernacle* is to have a *court*! Though not as large as the courtyards of temples that have been excavated, the measurements (*length . . . a hundred cubits, and the breadth fifty*) are of the order of 50 metres by 25 in modern measurements – not easy for a portable shrine. The furnishings of the court are comparable to those required earlier for the tabernacle itself.

27. 20–21   References to people have been lacking since 25. 8. Now, in a section marked out in the Masoretic Text of the Hebrew Bible as a new beginning, we have a preparation for the priestly requirements which will occupy chs 28–29. First a task is laid upon *the Israelites*. They are pictured here simply as minor members of a religious community, whose role is to maintain an adequate supply of olive *oil* for the *lamp*, presumably one of those described in 25. 37. This lamp is to burn all night, and the first, apparently rather modest, requirement laid upon the priestly families is to *keep the lamp in trim*. The ambitious scale of these requirements is reflected in that this is to be *binding . . . for all time*.

28. 1–5   Attention now focusses on those who are to minister in the sanctuary when it is completed. Moses' status as an intermediary between God and people is emphasized by the fact that those chosen are to be summoned *into your presence*. *Aaron* is pictured as the proto-typical *priest*, and all of his sons (already listed in 6. 23) are also to serve. It seems as if there were disputes between different groups claiming priestly status; *Nadab and Abihu* had accompanied Moses into the divine presence at 24. 9, but were disgraced according to a cryptic story in Leviticus 10. 1–2. *Eleazar and Ithamar* are not mentioned elsewhere in Exodus, but according to I Chron. 24 it was from their families that the priesthood of the Jerusalem temple was established. We may note more generally that there are many similarities between these chapters of Exodus and the account of David's preparations for the Jerusalem temple in I Chron. 22–28.

In the present context the priestly status of all of those listed is accepted, and the first concern is that they should be furnished with the proper vestments. What is required is outlined in vv. 4–5, and then spelt out in greater detail in the following sections. The proper clothes are here seen as giving their wearers *dignity and grandeur*, and the importance of appropriate clothing for particular occasions remains a persistent theme in many modern cultures; how far such concerns stem from the Hebrew Bible, and how far that Bible is itself a reflection of deeper human concerns is not easy to decide. The fate of the man without a wedding garment in Matt. 22. 11–13 shows that the New Testament shares these concerns.

28. 6–14   The first vestment described, *the ephod*, is also one of the most puzzling. Sometimes, as here, it appears to be an outer garment, made of precious materials, and showing the priest as the representative of all Israel. Though the word 'tribes' is not here used, that is the picture of the community of *the sons of Israel* which is envisaged. This picture, of the ephod as a garment, is consonant with the story of the child Samuel wearing a linen ephod as he went about his duties under Eli (I Sam. 2. 18). Elsewhere, however, the ephod appears to have been a cultic object (Judg. 8. 27; 17. 5). It might be possible to reconcile the two usages by supposing that the cultic object was characteristically decorated with priestly clothing, but this is no more than guesswork. Cultic usage in ancient Israel was probably very varied; the text in its final form has tried to impose uniformity, but glimpses of variety can still be traced.

28. 15–21   A 'breastpiece' had been mentioned (before the ephod) in the list of vestments as v. 4; now it is further characterized as *the breastpiece of judgment*. This rather cryptic expression should be read in

the light of v. 30, where reference is made to 'the Urim and the Thummim', which are to be put into it. Once again the representative function of the priest is stressed, as the twelve precious stones of the breastpiece *correspond to the twelve sons of Israel*. The symbolic use of twelve precious stones (the identity of some of which remains uncertain, as can be seen by reference to different translations) became a characteristic biblical theme right through to the end of the Book of Revelation where the stones picture 'new Jerusalem' (Rev. 21. 19–20).

28. 22–29   Instructions follow for the proper fastening of the *breastpiece* to the *ephod*. Symbolism well outweighs practicality here; though the section closes with a reference to *Aaron entering the holy place*, it is not at all clear that he would have been able to move when enclosed in so great a weight of precious material.

28. 30   References to *the Urim and the Thummim* are found in different parts of the Hebrew Bible, and their presence in *the breastpiece of judgment* shows that they were in some way intended to help the priest in reaching judicial decisions. The REB translators clearly had this understanding in mind with their expression *symbols of judgment*; the Hebrew actually only says that Aaron would 'bear the judgment'. The most common understanding of Urim and Thummim is that they functioned as some kind of lot, which might provide either a positive or a negative answer to questions that were put. (Or there may have been three possibilities: Yes, No, and No Answer, as could be implied by the story of Saul in I Sam. 28. 6.) They may have fallen out of use in the later biblical period (Ezra 2. 63), but all the references to them are rather allusive and we do not know the precise details of what was involved.

28. 31–35   We return to the ephod. The *mantle* was apparently some form of outer covering for it of a protective nature (*to prevent it tearing*). There follows the first biblical reference to the *pomegranate*. Later this is often found in descriptions of the priestly robes and temple ornamentation, as here and in I Kings 7, and also as a symbol of fertility, as in the Song of Songs. Whether these two usages were consciously connected we cannot be certain. The accompanying *bell* is given a more practical explanation: so that the movements of the priest in the dangerous setting of the sanctuary could be heard. The bell would also reassure God that the person entering the holy place was the legitimate priest.

28. 36–38   The intermediary role of the priest is brought out here. The *medallion* with its inscription served both as a kind of password, guaranteeing that its wearer was *acceptable to the* LORD, and also as a reminder to the people that any errors in their *rites* could be put right through the priestly ministration.

28. 39–44   V. 39 seems to stand somewhat apart, as a completion of the details of the priestly clothing. It is followed by the first reference to the robes for the remaining priests – here described as *Aaron's sons*, but it seems clear, especially from the requirement that this is to be a *statute binding . . . for all time*, that the continuing priestly orders were under consideration. Though they are to be given *dignity and grandeur*, their clothing was considerably less elaborate than what was required for Aaron himself earlier in the chapter, and there was more concern for modesty (*shorts . . . covering their private parts*) than for display. Though the term 'high priest' is not used in this chapter, it seems clear that the distinction which the author had in mind was that between the lesser priests and the high priest, who in the Second Temple period took on many of the characteristics, including the clothing, of a royal figure. It is instructive to read ch. 50 of Sirach (Ecclesiasticus), in the Apocrypha, for a picture of the impression created by the high priest.

29. 1–9a   The instructions in the previous chapter regularly began with 'Make'. In this chapter they start with *Take* (though the Hebrew uses a greater variety of forms of that verb than the repetition in REB might imply). An elaborate ceremony of *installation* is to be performed. We should not enquire too closely into the practicalities of what must have been a very unpleasant occasion: how were a *young bull and two rams* to be kept in order throughout the elaborate vesting ceremony performed over both *Aaron* and *his sons*? It is scarcely surprising that writers in the Hellenistic age, such as Philo and the author of the Letter to the Hebrews, preferred to concentrate on the symbolic meaning underlying such ceremonies.

29. 9b–14   Very precise rituals are now laid down for the *slaughter* of the *bull*, and the disposal of its bodily parts. Even allowing for great expertise on the part of the participants this must have been an extended procedure. We have no means of knowing, from the way in which the details are spelt out here, how many of the different functions could be performed simultaneously. Were the rams simply

to be held while the dismembering of the bull was carried out? In any case what we have here is in effect a brief outline of the rites which are to be spelt out in greater detail in Leviticus. Just as we have noted that some parts of this and other biblical books pose difficulties for women, so it cannot be easy for vegetarians to accept the world-view here envisaged with its mass slaughter of animals for human consumption.

29. 15–18   The way in which a *whole-offering* was to be offered is described much more fully in Lev. 1. REB's 'whole-offering' stresses the completeness of the gift; the translation 'burnt-offering' (NRSV and elsewhere) emphasizes rather the way in which the offering was made.

29. 19–21   Details with regard to *the second ram* are spelt out more precisely, for this is what will later be called 'the ram of installation'. It too is of course to be *slaughtered*, but whereas the blood of the first ram was flung against the sides of the altar, before that is done here *some of the blood* is to be applied to the extremities of the bodily parts of the candidates: *ears, thumbs and big toes*. The way in which this symbolized the whole body being devoted to God's service is clear enough; whether there was other, now more obscure, symbolism involved cannot now be known. In a rather curious – and surely impractical? – way, when the blood has been flung on *the altar*, it is to be taken again and *sprinkled* on the bodies and *vestments* of those being installed. The *anointing oil* had been mentioned at v. 7, and, together with the blood, it acted as a consecration of the candidates.

29. 22–25   In some rites those being installed were to eat appropriate parts of the sacrificial animals, and that point emerges at v. 26. It does not seem to be envisaged in this section, though we might have expected it to be so from the reference to the *loaf of bread, cake cooked with oil . . . and the wafer of unleavened bread*. Instead, all are offered to God and then burnt as a *whole-offering*. It is described as a *food-offering to the* LORD. Whether gods required food was a tricky subject in the ancient world. Frequent references in the Hebrew Bible to the bodily parts of God, and expressions like the present one, make it likely that it was at one time taken for granted that God required food; later this idea came to be rejected, and eventually was used as a way of mocking supposedly ignorant heathen. (The book in the Apocrypha, 'Daniel, Bel and the Snake', provides a humorous example of this polemic.)

29. 26–28   It now appears, however, contrary to what seemed to be the case previously, that one part of the *ram of installation* was to be treated differently. *The breast* was *presented* 'before' rather than 'to' the Lord, and thus remains available as *set aside* for *Aaron and his sons*. This is regularly to be the priestly perquisite. REB *contribution* may not quite catch the sense; it smacks too much of flag-days and church collections. It is that part of the people's total offering which is to be available to the priestly officiants.

29. 29–30   Provision is now made for the succession to *Aaron*. It is to be one *from among his sons*, and the chosen one is to wear the more elaborate vestments *for seven days*. As noted above the term 'high priest' is not used here, but the chosen one came to be understood in those terms, and an elaborate set of rules developed as to which functions were to be reserved to the high priest.

29. 31–34   Having a good appetite seems to be an essential require-ment of the priestly group. In addition to the breast set aside at v. 27, the laity are now warned that the *flesh* of the *ram of installation* and *the bread* are reserved for priestly consumption. A whole theology, of food and of the way in which material things are sanctified, is implicit here. At the practical level, it may be that it was easiest to dispose of the excess by *fire*.

29. 35   This verse can be treated as a summary of the preceding requirements, but it is also possible to see it as introducing the next section, in which what has so far appeared to be a one-off ceremony is to be repeated for *seven days*.

29. 36–37   Though treated now as integral to the installation ceremony, it looks as if the rite described here may originally have been independent of it, and linked by reference to the *bull* here and the rams in v. 38. In this section the emphasis is on *expiation for sin*, and we have one of the clearest examples in the whole Hebrew Bible of the way in which 'holiness' was regarded as contagious. Once *the altar* was *consecrated* it became *most holy* and *whoever touches* it receives its holiness. We need to remember that the whole idea of holiness has radically changed in modern usage; now it is probably most often used of the quality of an individual's life. But in the biblical world holiness was a condition, so that whereas nowadays 'to be holy' and 'to be unclean' would be concepts far

apart from one another, in the Hebrew Bible they are very closely related.

29. 38–46   The description of the ceremony concludes with instructions for offering the *rams*. It is not clear why REB translation changes, with 'ram' in vv. 38–39, 41 and 'lamb' in v. 40; the same Hebrew word is used throughout. For another difficulty of usage, however, the translators cannot be criticized; thus far 'you' has been singular and has referred to Moses. From v. 42 onwards the 'you' is plural, and the whole assembly seems to be envisaged. The last four verses read like a conclusion, stressing that *the Tent of Meeting* is set apart as the place where God will encounter the community, and reiterating the special priestly status of *Aaron and his sons*. More generally God will be with the community and *will become their God*. Again the translation can be criticized here, for this might imply something new. Something like 'continue to be their God' would bring out the sense. Finally the preceding section is placed in the context of the whole book of Exodus by the reminder that this is the *God who brought them out of Egypt*.

30. 1–10   The last part of ch. 29 seemed to be a conclusion, but there are more ritual requirements to be spelt out. First, the *altar* mentioned in ch. 27 is described in greater detail. The practical difficulties of a wooden altar remain, though they are less acute here as this is specifically an altar *to burn incense*. Its decoration is described; the fact that it is portable is stressed, and its appropriate position *in front of the Ark of the Testimony* laid down. This description of the place of encounter has not been used since ch. 26, but clearly in the minds of the final compiler it was synonymous with the Tent of Meeting.

Incense had an important symbolic role in Israelite worship, and many finds in archaeological excavations have been identified as incense altars or incense burners. It may also have had practical value, the odour of incense masking the smell of the animal sacrifices, but its importance clearly went beyond that. We do not know what may have constituted *unauthorized incense*, but it was a matter of great seriousness, and it was for offering such incense that Nadab and Abihu were condemned in Lev. 10, and the company of Korah in Num. 16.

30. 11–16   The next command is unexpected. Elsewhere in the Hebrew Bible to *take a census* is a wrong action (II Sam. 24); here it seems to be required in an entirely matter-of-fact way. But it is clear

that here also it was regarded as requiring proper ritual precautions, *to avert plague*. A standard *contribution* is required as a kind of poll-tax, with the same amount required of each, *rich and poor*. The proceeds are to be given to *the service of the Tent of Meeting*. Matt. 17. 24–27 refers to this tax; it is disputed whether that curious little episode shows that the tax was still collected in Jesus' time or whether it should be understood rather as a brief comment on a scriptural text.

30. 17–21   The dangers implicit in divine worship are once again prominent. It was no doubt appropriate that those about to enter *the Tent of Meeting* or *approach the altar* should *wash with water*, but we may feel it excessive that neglect of this requirement should be expressed as if it were a capital offence: *lest they die*. What is expressed here is a fear of the consequences of impurity, with the risk that the holiness of tent and altar might contaminate the priests with fatal results. It may also have been a way in which the priests stressed their own status and responsibilities.

30. 22–33   There have been previous references to *anointing oil*, but so far it has simply been taken for granted. Now detailed instructions for its preparation are provided, from a variety of herbs and *olive oil*, in a unique recipe not to be imitated for secular purposes. This specially prepared oil is then to be used for anointing all the furniture whose construction has been required, together with *Aaron and his sons*, whose priestly status is once again established. No indication is given how often this ceremony was to be repeated; it is described as a once-for-all occasion without the 'throughout your generations' instructions found elsewhere.

30. 34–38   The preparation of *incense* is laid down in similar terms, though with less precision as to quantities (*'some of it'*). But again a clear distinction is to be maintained between holy and personal use, with the threat, as in v. 33, that wrong use of the preparation will lead to the offender being *cut off from his father's kin* – in effect excommunicated from the worshipping community.

31. 1–11   Reference is now made to someone previously unmentioned: *Bezalel*. The *Hur* here mentioned as his grandfather might be the same as the character with the supporting role in 17. 8–13, but the link is not made, and the earlier figure was never said to be *of the tribe of Judah*. Bezalel is said to be *filled . . . with the spirit of God*. The 'spirit of

God' should not too readily be linked with Christian beliefs concerning the Holy Spirit. Rather, it is the instrument of creation in Gen. 1. 2, and using the expression here brings out the creative power given to Bezalel. Here it involves *workmanship of every kind*, an appropriate parallel at the human level to the total work of creation carried out by God. *His assistant* is to be *Aholiab*; he comes from *the tribe of Dan*, usually one of the least considered groups. It is noteworthy that the account of the building of Solomon's temple in II Chronicles also features the 'son of a Danite woman' (II Chron. 2. 14). The versatility of these two is remarkable, for they are to superintend the construction of all that has been described in the preceding six chapters. Fortunately they do not have to do it all themselves; they will be assisted by *every skilled craftsman*. Once again we are reminded that this picture of the Israelite community is very different from the group of agriculturalists who had escaped from Egypt.

31. 12–17   Just as Bezalel's endowment with the spirit of God recalled the beginning of the creation story, so the emphasis on *the Sabbath* recalls its end, as is specifically brought out at v. 17. Punishment is laid down for what is regarded as *profaning* the Sabbath: either death or at the least to be *cut off* from one's clan. Sections like this provide some of the explanation for the bitter divisions in the modern state of Israel between those 'orthodox' groups who try to insist on such observance and the majority who regard the Sabbath in a much more relaxed way.

31. 18   The lengthy instructions of God to Moses conclude with a link verse. The reference to *the Testimony* recalls 25. 16, and the long series of ritual laws; the reference to the *two tablets* fulfils the promise made at 24. 12. The tablets will also be very prominent in the narrative that is to follow. The final composition of Exodus is a much more skilful affair than one might suppose from those accounts which simply regard it as a patchwork of different literary sources.

The Israelites' apostasy
   32. 1–33. 23

32. 1–6   This compositional skill is again revealed here. The ritual laws of chs 25–31 have been spelt out in great detail, and – tedious as they may appear to many modern readers – they have played an

important part in establishing the religious practices of the community. But their very length makes credible the impatience of *the people*, though it does not excuse it. They make a basic mistake straightaway, when they speak of *this Moses, who brought us up from Egypt*. Of course it was not Moses but God who brought them up from Egypt! With so basic a misunderstanding it is not surprising that they should seek fresh *gods to go before us*.

There follows one of the most extraordinary episodes in the whole story. *Aaron* is an elusive figure, but he is usually pictured as fulfilling the priestly role, and is thus greatly venerated. In this story, by contrast, he is presented not just as an inadequate leader but also as a rather absurd figure. He demands the women's *gold rings*. Where a fugitive group would have acquired such rings is not stated; Jewish tradition links this episode with the 'spoiling of the Egyptians' theme in 12. 35–36 and elsewhere, but this is not mentioned in our story. There follows a direct contravention of the commandments laid down in 20. 4–6, forbidding the making of an *image* of the kind here described. Further, the image is that *of a bull-calf*. Gods were often depicted in bull-like forms in the Ancient Near East, but Israel came to reject any representation of its God, and that is a theme which is prominent in the remainder of this episode. Apparently in some way more than one god is involved. The Hebrew word for 'god', *elohim*, is plural in form but can be singular in meaning, so that Yahweh himself can be described as *elohim*. Here, however, the pronoun *these* certainly suggests a plurality of gods. The situation is further complicated by the announcement of *a feast to the* LORD, as if they are still worshippers of Yahweh rather than of any different god(s) represented by the image.

It is important that this episode should be read in conjunction with the strikingly similar story in I Kings 12. 25–33, where Jeroboam king of Israel is pictured as acting in a way very like what is set out here. If Ex. 25–31 can be seen in broad terms as describing what were envisaged as the proper worship practices of the Jerusalem temple, then the parallel becomes stronger still, for the preceding chapters of I Kings had been concerned with the establishment of the temple and its worship. So in each story a false alternative to true worship is being set out, no doubt as a warning. The oddity of Aaron's discreditable role remains, and no satisfactory explanation of this has ever been established. All we can say is that rivalry within the priesthood did not spare the very head of that priesthood.

V. 6b has no parallel in the I Kings story, but provides an important link with what is to follow here. *Revelry*, we shall soon discover, is not a matter of innocent relaxation following the completion of the religious rites. Instead, there is an implicit link with the picture offered later in the Pentateuch of the kind of worship offered to their gods by the Canaanites, the present inhabitants of the Promised Land. The alleged depravity of Canaanite worship is largely a figment of Deuteronomistic imagination, but it is very probable that that is the comparison invited here.

32. 7–10   The scene changes. We are taken back to *the* LORD and *Moses* at the top of the mountain. Yahweh is envisaged as the all-knowing God, so that he is aware of what is going on among the people, but Moses remains ignorant. Just as in v. 1 the people had in effect repudiated God by saying that Moses had brought them from Egypt, now with a nice irony Yahweh repudiates his people by saying to Moses that they are *your people, the people you brought up from Egypt*. His verdict is that he will *put an end* to the people and in some unspecified way *make a great nation spring from* Moses. This threat will occur more than once in chs 32–34.

32. 11–14   The risk that God might repudiate his people is the most serious threat of all, so Moses addresses that problem first. He reminds Yahweh that it was he who *brought* the people *out of Egypt*. Moses has it right, where both God and the people had it wrong! Then Moses adduces two arguments. First, an interesting form of the argument still often employed in a variety of circumstances, 'What will the neighbours think?' The neighbours here are *the Egyptians* who are pictured as seeing an explanation of their own misfortune in the even greater misfortune brought on the Israelites. This sheds interesting light on the threat which in the ancient world gods were thought to pose to friend and foe alike. Then secondly, in one of the relatively few links with the Genesis tradition, Moses recalls God's earlier promise to *Abraham, Isaac and Israel*, that they would be blessed with countless descendants and possession of the promised land. So *the* LORD changed his mind; the threat of *evil* is averted, at least for the moment.

32. 15–20   Now the two scenes are combined, with *Moses* descending the mountain with *the two tablets of the testimony*. Their great import-ance is emphasized: written on *both sides, the handiwork of God*, with God's own writing. There used to be much speculation whether God

actually wrote in Hebrew. We shall never know, because of the next dramatic development. *Joshua* had been reported as going up the mountain with Moses at 24. 13; as a layman he had not been involved in the instructions given in chs 25–31. Now he supposes that *fighting* has broken out *in the camp*, but *Moses* knows better. The seriousness of the situation is underlined by his bursting into a poetic fragment, with emphasis on the three-times repeated word *sound*. What they have heard they soon come to see. The image of *the bull-calf* is clearly prominently displayed, and the revelry of which we heard in v. 6 manifests itself in *dancing*.

Moses had sometimes been pictured earlier in the story as lacking in self-confidence, relying excessively on the guidance of others. Nothing of that here. His *anger* is roused; he *shattered* the precious *tablets*, *burnt* the image of the *calf*, grinding its remains *to powder*, and then made *the Israelites drink* water contaminated by the powder. This is clearly a story told for maximum dramatic effect, and we are not meant to concern ourselves with the logistics: how exactly one could shatter stone tablets in a sudden fit of anger; how an image largely made of gold rings could so readily be burnt; how six hundred thousand people could be forced to drink. Points of this kind are not the concern of the writer; the dramatic action is the key, and it brings out a very important aspect of the religion of ancient Israel. There was clearly a movement which we might describe as 'Puritan', opposed to revelry and what was regarded as licentiousness in religious practice. That movement eventually prevailed within large parts of the Judaeo-Christian tradition, and this whole chapter is a classic presentation of its ideals. Revelry, dancing, and the like are regarded as incompatible with true worship. It is a dispute which is far from over in many different religious traditions.

32. 21–24   There follows one of the most classic examples of 'passing the buck' to be found in any literature. Though God's instructions to Moses on the mountain had largely concerned *Aaron*, he had not been present; he had been left in charge of the people below (24. 13). Moses first supposes that the people had put unbearable pressure on him, but that he must bear responsibility for the *guilt* that had accrued. Aaron's immediate and oh-so-human response is to blame everyone else: *You know how wicked the people are.* It is all their fault. Moses is once again pictured as if he rather than God had *brought* them *up from Egypt*; he had disappeared up the mountain and so they were leader-less. Aaron admits that he had told them to provide the *gold*, which he

had thrown *in the fire*. And then: *out came this bull-calf*! It is as if the image had created itself, without anyone being responsible for it. And of the subsequent revelry not a word is said. It is astonishing, and in some ways rather reassuring, that the tradition represented by the Hebrew Bible with its great respect for Aaron should have allowed such a story to be told.

32. 25–29   The punishment of being forced to drink contaminated water is either forgotten or regarded as inadequate. Still *the people were out of control*. That is clear enough; much less clear is the following clause, that they were now *open to the secret malice of their enemies*. This might be a reference back to the Egyptians, as at v. 12, but the main point seems to be to stress the responsibility of *Aaron* for the disaster which is to follow. It is striking that, despite the readiness of Exodus to lay down punishments for all kinds of offences, Aaron here remains completely unpunished. Instead, punishment is to be meted out to the people. In response to Moses' appeal for loyalty, *the Levites all rallied to him*, and they are then empowered to carry out a form of ritual slaughter of *brother, friend, neighbour*, so that *about three thousand of the people died that day*. As the story is told, the killing seems almost incidental; its main purpose is apparently to validate the role of the Levites. Moses was himself a Levite (2. 1), but that seems irrelevant here. Rather, these verses offer us an extreme picture of what is involved in being committed to the Lord's service. Just as Jesus, in a way rather embarrassing for Christians, tells potential disciples that they must hate their family (Luke 14. 26), so here we have that 'hatred' turned into drastic action. It must seem ironic to the modern reader that such savagery can be described as *having brought a blessing upon yourselves*.

The end result is that the Levites *have been installed as priests*. This is slightly unexpected. The Book of Deuteronomy has frequent references to 'the priests, the Levites' (e.g. 17. 18: REB prefers to render the expression as 'levitical priests'), but in Exodus, Leviticus and Numbers it is normally stressed that only the family of Aaron might exercise the priesthood. Traditional source critics have detected different strata here; however that may be, both the literary tension and the violence involved in this story remind us that the office of priesthood was a hotly disputed matter in ancient Israel.

32. 30–35   This section is divided into two units by REB, but is better taken as a whole. In it a new role for *Moses* comes to the fore: that

of intercessor. Once again he goes up the mountain, on his own initiative, without being summoned. This time he is to act as an intermediary. The people (actually *this people,* a frequent way of speaking of a community in a slighting way) have committed *a great sin.* No suggestion is made that their repentance should be required as a precondition; instead Moses announces that unless God does *forgive* he wants no further part in the action. REB here has expanded the Hebrew text by adding the word *forgive* a second time; the Hebrew simply has 'If you will forgive their sins . . .' (cf. NRSV). This is a subtle form of blackmail, we may feel, in view of the promise of God at vv. 9–10. The divine verdict is in effect a suspended sentence. First, we have reference to a kind of record *book,* already mentioned by Moses. Whoever is *blotted out* of that book will simply disappear from human record. Moses will not be blotted out, but the sinners among the people, presumably in particular the three thousand victims of the Levites, will. Next, the promise of an accompanying *angel,* made in 23. 20, 23, is reiterated. Despite all that has happened God's promise still holds. But finally, the threat of further punishment remains. Both the Hebrew and most English translations are ambivalent whether *their sin* is a reference to the wrongdoings already committed or to the inevitability of future sin. And so the chapter closes with both *the people* and *Aaron* being held responsible for what may be regarded as the greatest wrong of all: the idolatry involved in *the bull-calf.* Later Jewish reflection came to see Moses here as acting as a substitute by whom the sins of the community were borne, but this may be a conscious reaction to Christian claims on behalf of Jesus rather than anything which arises directly from the text.

33. 1–6   At first it seems as if the next divine message is an encouraging one. The stay at Sinai is now to come to an end; they are to *set out.* God's promises to *Abraham, Isaac and Jacob* are recalled, the presence of the *angel* is once again promised, and the existing inhabitants of *the land* are to be driven out. (There seems to be no special significance in the variation of the usual order, with *Amorites* here before *Hittites.*) But the reference to Moses as the one who *brought them up from Egypt* is something we have already seen to be ominous, and that is now spelt out more precisely. God will *not journey in your company,* because he cannot trust himself not to *destroy* them on account of their stubbornness. The angel is now pictured as being in effect a substitute for God, whereas earlier the angel had been envisaged as a manifestation of the divine presence. This is an occasion for mourning among

the people, symbolized by not wearing *ornaments*. The word here used has not occurred earlier in Exodus; presumably it was common knowledge that anyone not wearing any ornaments was in mourning. Their whole journey is thus pictured as a mourning procession, for they wore the ornaments *no more*. Their journey is here described as being *from Mount Horeb*. This is the third and last time in Exodus (cf. 3. 1; 17. 6) that this name is used for the mountain more generally known as Sinai. It has commonly been regarded as a sign of a different source, but if that is so it is curious that the final editor of the book took no notice of such an anomaly. Possibly its use here is to form an inclusio with ch. 3, where God's presence had first been manifested; but certainty is impossible.

33. 7–11 The regular narrative structure of the Hebrew is broken at this point, and REB, in common with other versions and probably rightly, sees this as suggesting habitual action (*used to take*) rather than the kind of one-off event previously described. The *Tent of Meeting* has been referred to several times within chs 25–31 (e.g. 27. 21), but its purpose has not previously been described in detail. Here we learn that it was a place of encounter (meeting) between God and Moses. Whereas some ways of describing the divine-human encounter (the tabernacle, the ark) seem to have envisaged it in terms of God's continual presence within the holy place, here it is pictured in more intermittent terms. God is present when *the pillar of cloud descends*. Appropriate ritual actions were to be carried out by *all the people*, now pictured once again as a religious community; the vast numbers envisaged in some parts of our story could scarcely *all rise and stand* and then *all prostrate themselves*.

V. 11 contains a very important theological assertion. *The LORD used to speak with Moses face to face*. The REB translation of the next phrase, *as one man speaks to another* is an adequate rendering of the Hebrew, but it loses something of the force of the traditional, 'as one speaks to a friend' (NRSV). The assertion says as much about Moses' status as about God's more general manifestation to human beings. Moses is here pictured as holding more than normal human status, as is shown by his intimacy with God. This presentation corresponds well with the direct instructions given to Moses on the mountain in chs 25–31; it is very much at odds with a different picture, which is exemplified by Num. 20. There Moses' actions are described as so displeasing to God that he was not to be allowed to enter the Promised Land. The section ends with the curious statement that Moses' *attendant, Joshua* was on permanent guard duty within *the Tent*. Such a statement is intended to stress the importance of the tent, where God made his appearance, rather than to be taken as a literal statement of fact.

33. 12–17   The remainder of the chapter is devoted to describing a further encounter between God and Moses, for which no precise context is given. In this section it might seem most natural to suppose that we are still in the Tent of Meeting, but the next section refers to a rock with a crevice, which implies quite a different setting. The fact of the encounter, rather than its locale, is paramount in the author's mind.

Moses' words to *the LORD* seem rather querulous; indeed they once again could be seen, particularly at vv. 15–16, as a mild form of blackmail. First, he complains about not being told *whom you will send with me*. It is not obvious what kind of answer this criticism expects. If it is a companion for Moses himself, then both Aaron and Joshua have been set aside in different ways. If it is a guide for the whole community, there have been repeated references (most recently in v. 2 of this chapter) to an angel who would accompany the people. Perhaps the underlying fear which prompted the question was that Yahweh was the God of Sinai; the people were now to leave that area, so could Yahweh continue to accompany and guide them in their continuing travels? Certainly that seems to be the concern which is answered at v. 14: *I shall go myself and set your mind at rest*. Before that, however, we have another outburst from Moses, demanding from God that he *teach me to know your ways*. Since the whole section from ch. 20 onwards has been devoted to precisely that, this seems a little excessive, but it provides a context for the next chapter in which further divine commands will be set out.

The point about God not being confined to the mountain is taken further in vv. 15–16. Once again Moses uses the same type of argument as he had employed at 32. 11–13. God will, as it were, let himself down if he does not accompany the people. If he fails in this, then *how can it ever be known* what he has done for his people? Moses is pictured as concerned for his own reputation and also for that of the people; only through God's continuing presence will it be recognized that they will be *distinct, I and your people, from all the peoples on earth*. This claim to a distinct position of favour with God has been implicit in much that has gone before in our story; it has not often been expressed so specifically as this. But Moses has proved himself to be a shrewd negotiator. God will *do what you have asked*, both in general terms because of Moses having *found favour*, and more specifically because

I know you by name. These two expressions recall v. 12, where they were also found, and thus form an inclusio within this short passage. But the reference to 'knowing by name' also provides an important connection with what is to follow. Just as Moses is known personally ('by name'), so in the next section God will reveal his name.

33. 18–23 The theological richness of this section continues, with a variety of ways of expressing the divine nature. First *Moses prayed.* The verb used is the ordinary one of speech, but it is followed by an intensive particle, so that the sense of prayer is appropriate. The request is for a vision of God's *glory.* This is a term not previously used in quite this sense in Exodus, though it was hinted at in 24. 16–17. It is a recognized way of expressing the divine presence in the Hebrew Bible; in particular the Book of Ezekiel starts with a vivid account of the 'appearance of the glory of the LORD' (Ezek. 1. 28), and later describes the departure of the 'Glory' from God's people and then later its return.

Next comes the emphasis on the divine *name*, which provides an obvious link back to chs 3 and 6. It may not be too fanciful to suppose that the deliberate mystery of the divine self-revelation in ch. 3 has been mitigated somewhat, by God's promise that *I will make all my goodness pass before you.* At least to Moses some fuller picture of the divine character is being offered. But the limits of God's being *gracious* and showing *compassion* are very much a matter of God's own decision, as Paul noted when quoting this verse at Rom. 9. 15.

The chapter ends with a specific act of self-revelation by God, which as already noted seems somewhat at odds with the earlier part of the chapter. The reference to *a crevice of the rock* is hardly compatible with the setting of the Tent of Meeting, and whereas earlier 'the LORD used to speak to Moses face to face' here *my face you cannot see.* Different traditions may well lie behind this material, but they have been woven together into a powerful description of God's presence with his chosen instrument.

The Covenant renewed
34. 1–34. 35

34. 1–9 For the moment the command to leave the mountain seems to have been set aside, and in fact not only the rest of Exodus, but also Leviticus and the first chapters of Numbers are still set at Sinai. The

first necessity is to repair the damage caused in the matter of the golden calf. So new *stone tablets* are to be prepared. This time *Moses* is to *cut* them, but the writing on the tablets is once again to be that of God himself. A problem follows. It is stated that the writing will be, as we might expect, *the words which were on the first tablets which you broke*. In the event this proves not to be the case; though there are some over-laps between what is set out in the rest of this chapter and what had already been described, the two sets of material are very far from being identical.

The unique status of Moses, already emphasized in ch. 33, is taken further here. This time *no one is to go up with you*, not even his faithful attendant Joshua. When he had yet again gone up the mountain, the LORD appeared to him and pronounced the divine name, seen once again as a means of knowing something of the divine nature. Here it is clear that the mountain is the place of the divine *presence*, rather than the Tent of Meeting as in ch. 33.

What follows is of great importance for the perception of God in ancient Israel. At first sight it seems curiously arranged in that it is presented as a piece of self-publicity from God. Vv. 6–7 have often been described as 'credal', and in a sense this is right, but one expects creeds to be proclaimed by worshippers rather than by the one being worshipped. However divine self-proclamation of this kind is not unusual in the religious literature of the Ancient Near East.

This assertion of the divine characteristics is one that is found with minor variations in many different parts of the Hebrew Bible, some-times in rather unexpected contexts. Thus, for example, Jonah uses the substance of this formula to blame God for not destroying Nineveh. For Jonah the trouble was that God was too 'gracious and compas-sionate' (Jonah 4. 2)! More conventionally, however, this is a standard way of expressing the received view of the divine character, and it can still be of value particularly for those modern readers who have convinced themselves of the harsh and unforgiving character of the God of the Old Testament.

Within the formula the demands of mercy and of justice are held in tension. Particular stress is placed on the word *ḥesed*, REB *faithful*, which is found in vv. 6 and 7. It is disputed whether the theme is specially linked to the notion of a covenant ('covenant love' has often been proposed as a translation), but the point stressed is certainly that of God's commitment to his worshippers. God's readiness to *forgive iniquity, rebellion and sin* is brought out, but alongside this comes the equal concern to emphasize that *the guilty* will receive their just rewards. This brings out what to the modern reader will be the least acceptable element in the formula: the punishment of *children and grandchildren . . . for the iniquity of their fathers*. There are few modern societies in which family solidarity goes that far.

The section ends with *Moses* showing proper respect in worship, and then raising once again the question of God's continuing presence with his people, which has been so much at question since the episode of the golden calf.

34. 10–16   The signs seem favourable. At once *the* LORD announces that he is *making a covenant*. Unexpectedly it is not stated that the covenant is to be with Israel, but the following description certainly implies that. *Miracles* are promised, the sense being more that of mighty works than of any acts which go beyond what we would call the laws of nature. In fact the only mighty work mentioned is the reiterated promise that God will *drive out* the existing *inhabitants of the land*. If that is to happen, it is not quite clear why the following instructions should be needed, but, in a manner reminiscent of Deuteronomy, the Israelites are very solemnly warned against the *snare* that those peoples would constitute. We are back in the un- attractive world of 'ethnic cleansing'. The emphasis is on the dangers inherent in alien religious practices, with the implication that to be involved with them also carried dangers to sexual standards. This is brought out by the word *wantonly*, and by the implication that to *partake of their sacrifices* may have as its consequence mixed marriages, and the Canaanite women *leading your sons astray*. The male perspec- tive is obvious enough; it is the *daughters going wantonly* who may *lead your sons astray*. Women are seen as a threat to the identity and purity of the community.

34. 17   What follows is a series of laws, whose connection with what has preceded seems to be just as slight as was that of the Decalogue in ch. 20. A tradition going back to the great German author and scholar Goethe has seen in what follows another Decalogue, and older studies often described these laws as a 'Ritual Decalogue', implicitly inviting comparison with the 'Ethical Decalogue' of ch. 20. Such a description is not very satisfactory; the following commands do not group themselves naturally into a series of ten, and the ritual concerns, though prominent, are not exclusive. In addition, the prohibition in this verse seems directly to reflect the episode of ch. 32. The words here used for *gods of cast metal* are found in 32. 4, 8, to

125

describe the golden calf. The dangers inherent in that episode were to shape the way in which the people understood and worshipped its true God.

34. 18 The requirements in vv. 18–26 are very close to those that have been set out already, some in 13. 13–14, others in 23. 12–19. This verse concentrates entirely on *Unleavened Bread*, as does 23. 15, so that it is rather unexpected to come across a quite separate reference to 'Passover' at v. 25. In the heyday of source criticism both the repetition in the larger unit and the two-fold reference to Unleavened Bread and Passover were seen as evidence that different sources had here been combined. This may be so, but it is also important to recognize how critical a part repetition plays in the shaping of the book of Exodus. Part of its dramatic effect is achieved by telling the same story, or laying down the same legal requirements, more than once. Similarly in the detailed point here, it is possible that we should see a deliberate literary device, this body of laws both beginning and ending with reference to the *pilgrim-feast* which commemorated the deliverance *from Egypt*. Either way it seems clear that this command looks back on the deliverance from a much later perspective.

34. 19–20 The parallel here is with 13. 12–15. The ambiguity that we noted there, where it might have been supposed that firstborn humans were to be devoted to Yahweh, is here avoided, with the requirement to *redeem every firstborn among your sons*.

34. 21 The Sabbath command is reiterated, though the name is not used, and it does not seem here to be very closely related to the surrounding laws. The obvious parallel is with 23. 12. There the emphasis was humanitarian, ensuring that all might rest, but with no reference to *ploughing time and harvest*. Their mention here is a clear indication that these commands reflected the customs of an established agricultural society.

34. 22–24 The reference to *those three times* appears at first to be a little misleading; the two *pilgrim-feasts* mentioned here are to be taken in conjunction with Unleavened Bread, mentioned in v. 18. The parallel is with 23. 16–17, but the command is elaborated here with a reference to God's saving acts. Not only will the other nations be *dispossessed* and the *frontiers extended*, but they will not even have to worry about the security of their homes when they leave them unoccupied to go to worship, for the *neighbours* will not be *covetous*. This is a curious contrast with the earthy realism of much else in Exodus, and the harsh criticisms of the community found in much of the prophetic material. It is interesting to note that the underlying assumption here is of all the males congregating for worship at a central sanctuary, as prescribed in Deuteronomy (ch. 12 and elsewhere) rather than joining together locally.

34. 25–26   These requirements closely parallel 23. 18–19, with the additional reference, already noted, to *Passover*.

34. 27–28   The statements in these two verses appear at first sight directly to contradict one another. V. 27 tells that Moses was to *write these words down*, and the reference must surely be to the commands that have just been set out in the preceding verses. V. 28, by contrast, says that the writing would be that of *the* LORD himself, and that the writing on the tablets was to be *the Ten Commandments*, that is, the Decalogue set out in ch. 20. REB's use of capitals seems to accentuate the discrepancy. Various solutions have been proposed; perhaps the most satisfactory understanding is to see the present section as being concluded at 28a (*'without food or drink'*), the remainder of the verse being a kind of appended note which brings the whole episode to an end with a reference back to ch. 20.

34. 29–32   Once more *Moses came down from Mount Sinai*, in happier circumstances than his descent in ch. 32. There is one more additional complication. Moses' proximity to God meant that *the skin of his face shone*. The context certainly demands a meaning such as 'shone', and this is accepted in most modern translations. It also seems to have been Paul's understanding in his reflection on this passage in II Cor. 3. 7–18. The usual meaning of the Hebrew verb, however, is 'to be horned', and there are various great Renaissance paintings of this episode which, following the Latin Bible, depict Moses with horns. Naturally *Aaron and the Israelites . . . were afraid*, but in this section Moses is able to reassure them and pass on to them *all the commands* he had received. Their content is not specified; we can think either of the brief summaries provided in the Decalogue and in vv. 17–26 of this chapter, or of the whole elaborate programme spelt out since they first arrived at Sinai in ch. 19.

34. 33–35   The last section had reinforced Moses' unique role, and

that is taken even further here. Now he is so imbued with God's presence that whenever he spoke with the people *he put a veil over his face*. Apparently he could talk with God face to face (cf. 33. 11), but it was dangerous for the ordinary people to have direct contact with Moses. This theme is brought out here to emphasize the remarkable status of Moses; it does not feature in the description of his actions in the remainder of the Pentateuch.

The building of the sanctuary
35. 1–40. 38

The greater part of these concluding chapters is devoted to description of the scrupulous carrying-out of the instructions given in chs 25–31. We noted above that the content of those chapters may seem somewhat tedious to modern readers; the repetition of that content in equally precise detail will not endear them any more. No attempt will be made in this commentary to work through each unit of these concluding chapters, but the significance of the repetition should not be overlooked. It is an important way for the compiler to emphasize the solemnity of God's commands.

35. 1–3   Every opportunity is taken to stress the importance of the *Sabbath*, which the compilers clearly saw as one of the most distinctive identity-markers of the community. In the first setting out of the ritual laws in chs 25–31 Sabbath observance had formed the conclusion and climax (31. 12–17); now it is stressed in a different way by being put first of all the commandments. It is the basic requirement of membership of the community. Breach of the commandment is again laid down as a capital offence, and now a specific example of such breach is given: *you are not even to light your fire*. It is the literal adherence to this form of the Sabbath requirement that explains the violence of some contemporary Orthodox Jews in Jerusalem against what they regard as the breaking of divine requirements.

35. 4–9   Anticipating the elaborate construction work that will be required, *Moses* now tells *the whole Israelite community* to prepare material. In theory the *contribution* is voluntary (*Let all who wish*), but in practice, as often in such circumstances, it is assumed that everyone will feel obliged to participate (*Each of you is to*). The setting is in any case extremely artificial; most of the material which is specified is not

the kind of thing which members of the community might happen to have available as a contribution. Rather, this is a repetition of 25. 2–7.

35. 10–19   There is no equivalent to this in the earlier commands. Indeed, there scarcely could have been, for this requirement of all *the skilled craftsmen* is a subsequent working out of the earlier commands. The material that they are to work with has, however, already been specified.

35. 20–29   Another section which is without parallel in more than one sense. It is so in that it is a sequel to God's earlier commands, but it is also remarkable in the picture of eager obedience to divine commands which it offers us. The community is time and again pictured as uncomprehending, resentful, querulous; here it is a story of *every Israelite man and woman who was minded to bring offerings* doing so freely. Sometimes this kind of ideal picture serves as a prelude to the description of a group of malcontents. Not so here; all is sweetness and light.

35. 30–36. 7   The appointment of *Bezalel and Aholiab* was already anticipated in 31. 1–11. What is new here is in line with the idealized picture of the community in the preceding section. Their generosity had already been mentioned; now it is so great that they *are bringing much more than we need*. It is rare indeed, in the ancient world or the modern, for religious leaders to tell their followers not to bring *anything more as a contribution for the sanctuary*.

36. 8–38   The instructions given in ch. 26 are now carried out. The constant repetition of *they made* as against the command 'make' given to Moses on the mountain is another way of emphasizing the obedience and loyalty of the community.

37. 1–39. 31   These three chapters are mainly concerned with the fulfilment of the instructions given in chs 25, 27 and 28, but the requirements of ch. 30 relating to the altar of incense, which we noted there to be a somewhat anomalous addition to the main body of laws, are here incorporated into their more natural place.

39. 32–43   The work has now been completed. Sometimes the construction has been described as a tabernacle, sometimes as a tent of meeting; here the two descriptions are neatly combined with the

phrase *Tabernacle of the Tent of Meeting*, but the main emphasis, at both the beginning and end of this section, is that *the Israelites did everything exactly as the* LORD *had commanded Moses.* The intervening verses provide a kind of inventory of the materials used. REB translation of v. 43 is unfortunate in that it obscures an important parallel. The Hebrew could be literally rendered 'Moses saw all the work and they had indeed done it as the LORD had commanded.' This is reminiscent of the work of creation described in Gen. 1. 1–2. 3. The importance of the tabernacle is stressed by picturing it as a creation in little.

40. 1–33a   The instructions so far given have in effect been timeless. But the regular round of a ritual calendar is important in religious observance. Here therefore the completed construction and all its furniture is to be *set up on the first day of the first month.* This provides two important links. First, we are reminded that the Passover offering coincident with the deliverance from Egypt had also taken place in the first month (12. 1). Secondly, this concern with beginning provides a further link with the creation story of Gen. 1. Now we have reached *the second year* (v. 17). The first part of this chapter, vv. 1–15, therefore consists of a series of imperatives to Moses. Then we are told that he *did everything exactly as the* LORD *commanded him.*

40. 33b–38   The book ends on a confident note. First we are assured that *Moses completed the work.* Then, after all the uncertainties relating to the divine presence with the people – would the Lord go with them or not? – we are told that *the glory of the* LORD *filled the Tabernacle.* In language reminiscent of the description of the departure from Egypt *the cloud by day . . . and the fire by night* accompany the people. It is a happy conclusion after all the anxieties of the book. But we also realize that the story is as yet incomplete. The last word of the book is *journey*, which we are surely meant to see as an allusion both to the people's continuing journey through the wilderness and the larger-scale journey of faith of which Exodus has provided a model.

.